Savory Pork Roast (see page 61)

Hot Caribbean Beans and Rice (see page 115)

Sicilian Grilled Chicken & Garlic (see page 78)

Crispy Parmesan Fried Chicken (see page 93)

Grilled Swordfish with Tomato-Dill Relish (see page 57)

Pan-Pacific Stir-Fry Beef (see page 15)

French Three-Onion Soup (see page 105)

Blackberry Cobbler (see page 161)

# Quick Family Meals ...In No Time

Robin Taylor Swatt

que

800 East 96th Street,
Indianapolis, Indiana 46290

# Quick Family Meals In No Time

International Standard Book Number: 0-7897-3299-8

Library of Congress Catalog Card Number: 2004109549

Printed in the United States of America

First Printing: October 2004

07  06  05  04          4  3  2  1

## Trademarks

## Warning and Disclaimer

## Bulk Sales

Que Publishing offers excellent discounts on this book when ordered in quantity for bulk purchases or special sales. For more information, please contact

**U.S. Corporate and Government Sales**
**1-800-382-3419**
**corpsales@pearsontechgroup.com**

For sales outside the United States, please contact

**International Sales**
**international@pearsoned.com**

**Executive Editor**
Candace Hall

**Development Editor**
Lorna Gentry

**Managing Editor**
Charlotte Clapp

**Copy Editor**
Jenny Matlik

**Indexer**
Ken Della Penta

**Publishing Coordinator**
Cindy Teeters

**Interior Designer**
Anne Jones

**Cover Designer**
Anne Jones

**Cover Illustrator**
Nathan Clement

**Page Layout**
Melanie Haage Design

# Table of Contents

# About the Author

**Robin Taylor Swatt** is a writer, educator, and former co-owner of Sacramento-based Savory Fare Catering. She is an elementary school teacher and author of 3 cookbooks. She also consults in the food services industry. Robin resides with her family in Sacramento, California.

# Dedication

*I would like to dedicate this to my wonderful family for truly knowing the importance of home-cooked, family meals. It is through them that I can appreciate the amazing discussions and togetherness that have always centered about the dining table. I also thank my husband, Jeff, for striving to develop more culinary skills in the kitchen so we can jointly produce quick and delicious meals for our family. And, lastly, I want to thank my network of girlfriends – strong, professional, working women –who daily understand the sensibility of quick-cooking and who have given me exceptional feedback on this cookbook.*

# We Want to Hear from You!

As the reader of this book, *you* are our most important critic and commentator. We value your opinion and want to know what we're doing right, what we could do better, what areas you'd like to see us publish in, and any other words of wisdom you're willing to pass our way.

As an executive editor for Que, I welcome your comments. You can email or write me directly to let me know what you did or didn't like about this book—as well as what we can do to make our books better.

*Please note that I cannot help you with technical problems related to the topic of this book. We do have a User Services group, however, where I will forward specific technical questions related to the book.*

When you write, please be sure to include this book's title and author as well as your name, email address, and phone number. I will carefully review your comments and share them with the author and editors who worked on the book.

**Email:**    feedback@quepublishing.com

**Mail:**    Candace Hall
Executive Editor
Que Publishing
800 East 96th Street
Indianapolis, IN 46240 USA

For more information about this book or another Que Publishing title, visit our Web site at www.quepublishing.com. Type the ISBN (0789732998) or the title of a book in the Search field to find the page you're looking for.

# Introduction

This is a typical scene across America: You're a working parent with many responsibilities. First, your children are clamoring for your attention with school forms to sign, homework for you to supervise, and the latest clash with their friends to vent to you. Then your spouse comes home from a tough day at work, wanting you to listen to his or her latest career problem. But don't forget your own workplace issues and responsibilities! Your boss may have given you work to take home or an important deadline may be looming. And when are you going to walk the dog? Attend the PTA meeting? Wash the laundry? Wrap that birthday gift? Make that important phone call? Pay that overdue bill? All this is on your mind, and you still need to get dinner on the table!

Even if you don't have the kids and the spouse, it is tempting just to run to the nearest fast food restaurant or heat up a frozen pizza. Yet, you know that you don't want to consume all that fat and spend all that money. Instinctively, you know that there must be a better way. But how can you balance your busy life with the time it takes to make a tasty, home-cooked meal? Is it even possible?

# Why Is a Home-Cooked Meal So Important?

Multiple studies have shown that home-cooking is healthier than consuming fast food. You can gain more control over the ingredients in whatever you make, alter a recipe to reflect your personal taste or dietary restrictions, focus on freshness and taste, and control the portion size.

In addition, a home-cooked meal lends itself to eating together as a family. Rather than madly chowing down on those fast food hamburgers in the car, you and your family can sit together around the dining table and decompress after a long day. Families communicate better while eating together. Dinnertime is a fantastic occasion to catch up on each other's activities and talk about tomorrow's plans. In this way, family ties are strengthened.

Studies also show that eating dinner together as a family affects children's academic achievement and social development. High schoolers who regularly eat dinner with their family (four or more times a week) score significantly higher on school achievement tests and show higher levels of motivation. They are less likely to use drugs or alcohol or be depressed. Similarly, elementary schoolchildren do better academically at school when they share the majority of their meals with their family. They are better adjusted than peers whose families do not eat together. Also, preschoolers whose families share dinners together have higher language skills and oral vocabulary because they listen to more sophisticated conversations that take place across the dinner table. Their increased exposure to vocabulary and higher-level oral language positively affects their reading performance in school.

Having dinner together as a family provides parents with a wonderful opportunity to model nutrition and good eating habits. You can help your children look at food as vital nourishment rather than reward. Studies show that children who have dinner with their parents enjoy a healthier diet and have lower levels of obesity. Children who eat family, home-cooked dinners eat more fruits and vegetables and eat less fried food and saturated fats than peers who rarely eat with their families or eat convenience foods.

Regularly eating home-cooked meals is important to your children and yourself. But in this day and age of busy, overscheduled lives and the convenience of take-out foods, you have to make the conscious choice to prepare dinners at home. Home-cooking isn't an old-fashioned fantasy but a reality that's well within your grasp.

# How Does This Cookbook Help?

This cookbook provides you with the solution to making home-cooking possible. We have created a cooking system that will help you make dinner with a minimum of time and effort. Not only will you create a delicious meal that your entire family will love, you will do so in a streamlined, fuss-free manner. As you become more familiar with cooking shortcuts and quick tips, you will find yourself looking forward to cooking as a way to unwind from a stressful day. In addition, our cookbook demonstrates how you can involve the entire family in the food preparation process as well as provides you with an efficient shopping list to make your next trip to the grocery store unbelievably easy.

How is this cookbook different from others? Rather than just provide you with quick recipes for simple dishes with simple flavors, our cookbook specifically gives you shortcuts that abbreviate cooking time so that you can create real meals with sophisticated, layered flavors. In addition, for each recipe, we provide detailed ways that helpers can aid you in the kitchen. We also supply you with a comprehensive shopping list that names the specific food container sizes found in the grocery store that you will need to fulfill the requirements of each recipe. Finally, we give you a list of pantry items that will make your life even easier.

# What Will You Accomplish?

By the time you have created the dishes presented in this book, you will have an excellent foundation in quick cooking. You will be able to make delectable, practical meals fit for family or guests in a minimum amount of time. In addition, you will have a good grasp of flavor combinations and cooking shortcuts that will help you rapidly tackle any recipe you encounter. Rather than seeing cooking dinner as a chore, you will welcome the opportunity to employ your newfound cooking techniques and dazzle your family and friends with your culinary prowess.

This cookbook will also help you see cooking as an easy way to interact with your children. Your child helpers will learn about basic culinary techniques, food history, and fun food facts. They will enjoy being part of the culinary team and will take pleasure in helping to put dinner on the table. As you teach them about food and cooking, you will strengthen your relationship with your children and also make food preparation quicker and easier!

# Recipe Layout

As is the case with all cookbooks, each recipe is composed of a list of ingredients and instructions that show you how to make a particular dish. However, each recipe also includes some valuable additions to make your cooking experience particularly worthwhile:

Employing child help while cooking is a great way to multi-task. Not only are you spending quality time with your child, but your child is also making your food preparation quicker while learning valuable kitchen skills. Since one of the goals of this cookbook is to help busy parents create quick, fuss-free meals, I have included a very specific list of ways a child could help with each recipe. Of course, these "Helper Hints" always require adult supervision, and, in all cases, you will have to model specific food preparation techniques before letting your helper become fully independent with a child-safe task. However, with time and practice, your child will become a competent sous-chef in the kitchen, making your job as head chef so much easier. Who knows…you may even have a mini-Julia Child or James Beard in the making!

**Teachable Moment:** As a part of the "Helper Hints" section, this helps you to seize the opportunity to teach your child helper something fascinating about food and cooking. I have included some fun, kid-friendly facts about food and interesting food history. For example, your child can learn about the history of pizza, where chocolate comes from, and how maple syrup is made. This helps your child helper connect to each recipe, look to you as a mentor, and enjoy a more global view of cooking and food. By taking advantage of each opportunity for learning and interacting, you will strengthen the bonds between parent and child and keep cooking fun. And you may even find that you learn something new about food yourself!

## quick tip

Sometimes a recipe will lend itself to various shortcuts. By presenting these shortcuts, our goal is to preserve the high quality and luscious taste of each recipe while minimizing your time and effort. Each quick tip is meant to be practical, advantageous, and easy to accomplish.

# Your Shopping List:

For each recipe, we have included a shopping list that specifically details the items you need to buy. Before I became an experienced cook, it was frustrating to go to the store and try to determine which containers I needed to fulfill the requirements of a recipe. Therefore, I created this list so that you will know exactly what items to buy and in which container sizes. All the guesswork has been eliminated!

## From Your Pantry:

Each recipe has a list that includes items you should already have in your kitchen pantry. Always double check this list to make sure your pantry has all of these items before planning your shopping. You may need to add an item to your pantry or replenish something that you have used already.

## A Note about the Pantry and Food Shopping:

I have compiled a list of basic pantry needs that will help you create the quick, delicious meals in this cookbook. All of these pantry items can be found in your local supermarket. In addition to assisting you with the recipes in this publication, you will find that these multi-purpose items are essential to general cooking. This list is by no means comprehensive, but it will give you the central framework upon which to build your pantry stores. You will discover that once you have a well-equipped pantry, everyday cooking becomes much quicker and easier. Instead of running to the store for a last minute item, you can rest assured that you have an arsenal of ingredients from which to create delectable but speedy meals.

### Spices and Seasonings

**The Basics:**
- [ ] fresh garlic
- [ ] kosher salt
- [ ] black peppercorns (for grinding)
- [ ] dried oregano
- [ ] dried rosemary
- [ ] dried thyme
- [ ] dried tarragon
- [ ] celery seed powder
- [ ] dry onion flakes
- [ ] bay leaf
- [ ] ground cumin
- [ ] celery salt
- [ ] ground chili powder
- [ ] cayenne pepper
- [ ] red pepper flakes
- [ ] paprika
- [ ] dry mustard
- [ ] garlic powder
- [ ] fat-free butter-flavored sprinkles
- [ ] sesame seeds

## Baking Needs

- ❏ cornstarch
- ❏ cornmeal
- ❏ all-purpose flour
- ❏ prepared baking mix
- ❏ quick-cooking oats
- ❏ baking soda
- ❏ baking powder
- ❏ unsweetened cocoa
- ❏ sugar
- ❏ powdered sugar
- ❏ dark and light brown sugar
- ❏ light corn syrup
- ❏ dark and light molasses

## The Refrigerated Pantry

- ❏ unsalted butter
- ❏ margarine
- ❏ whole milk
- ❏ low fat milk

**These items can be stored in a cool, dark place before opening. Once opened, they must be refrigerated:**

- ❏ tomato paste in the tube
- ❏ hot pepper sauce
- ❏ prepared tartar sauce
- ❏ mayonnaise
- ❏ hot sweet mustard
- ❏ Dijon mustard
- ❏ catsup or ketchup
- ❏ prepared barbecue sauce
- ❏ prepared horseradish
- ❏ non-pareil capers
- ❏ prepared ranch salad dressing

## Oils, Vinegars, and Flavorings

**Make sure to store these oils, vinegars, and flavorings away from heat. They need to be kept in a cool, dry, dark place.**

**Oils:**
- ❏ extra-virgin olive oil
- ❏ sesame oil
- ❏ vegetable oil
- ❏ peanut oil
- ❏ cooking spray

**Vinegars:**
- ❏ red wine vinegar
- ❏ cider vinegar
- ❏ white vinegar
- ❏ balsamic vinegar

**Flavorings:**
- ❏ fresh garlic
- ❏ Worcestershire sauce
- ❏ fish sauce
- ❏ soy sauce
- ❏ dry white wine
- ❏ Kahlua® liquor
- ❏ rum
- ❏ honey
- ❏ pure maple syrup
- ❏ peanut butter

## Baking Flavorings

**These are particularly important for baking:**

- ☐ vanilla extract
- ☐ cream of tartar
- ☐ ground cinnamon
- ☐ ground allspice
- ☐ ground cloves
- ☐ ground nutmeg
- ☐ ground ginger

## Optional Items

**These are some other items that are in my personal pantry arsenal.**

- ☐ yellow or white onions
- ☐ new potatoes
- ☐ lemons
- ☐ limes
- ☐ couscous
- ☐ bottled salsas
- ☐ bottled chili sauce
- ☐ tamari sauce
- ☐ Asian-style garlic-chili paste
- ☐ pasta sauces
- ☐ curry mixes
- ☐ vegetable broth
- ☐ beef broth
- ☐ coconut milk
- ☐ Japanese panko breadcrumbs
- ☐ assorted canned beans
- ☐ eggs or egg substitute
- ☐ fresh parmesan cheese
- ☐ fresh ginger
- ☐ pesto
- ☐ frozen peas
- ☐ frozen kernel corn
- ☐ assorted nuts (I keep these in the freezer.)
- ☐ disposable aluminum casserole and baking pans (for freezing extras)

## Shortcut spices

**These seasonings are a combination of various spices:**

- ☐ seasoned salt
- ☐ garlic salt
- ☐ Caribbean jerk seasoning
- ☐ Cajun spice
- ☐ dried Italian seasoning
- ☐ dry onion soup mix

## The Shelf Pantry

- ☐ canned tomatoes
- ☐ canned tomato sauce
- ☐ refried beans
- ☐ assorted rice
- ☐ assorted pasta
- ☐ chicken broth
- ☐ beef buillon
- ☐ seasoned bread crumbs

## Handy Disposable Tools

- ❏ gallon-size resealable bags
- ❏ quart-size resealable bags
- ❏ aluminum foil
- ❏ plastic wrap
- ❏ paper towels

## Shopping and Pantry Tips:

Scope out the stores for items that are on sale. I always look for sale items in the meat and seafood departments and freeze them for later use. My freezer currently has chicken breasts, pork tenderloin, and prawns that I bought on sale.

Plan your meals in advance so that you only shop once. On Saturdays, I sit down and plan my family's dinners for the upcoming week, taking into account other dinner obligations. Then, I plan meals with a consideration for what I may already have on hand in my refrigerator, freezer, and pantry, and for what may be on sale at the local grocery stores. I create my shopping list and then go to the grocery store and farmer's market. When I come home from the store, I am confident that I have all the items I need for the week and will not have to rush to the store at the last minute.

Buy the highest quality items you can find. Seek out farmer's markets for quality produce. Ask your peers for their recommendations for grocery items.

Create personal relationships with your grocers and food suppliers. They will often point you to the best deal or suggest a new delicious food item you might not otherwise try. For example, the supermarket butcher may tell you that something has just gone on sale or is particularly fresh. They may even recommend tried and true recipes!

Buy bulk items from club stores only when you are sure they are a good deal. Be careful – sometimes it's easy to miscalculate and buy the club store bulk item when it's actually cheaper elsewhere.

Make sure you only buy what you can store and use before the item goes bad. For example, I would go to the local club store and buy a huge bag of spinach leaves because it was offered at such an incredible price per pound. At home, I would have to rearrange items in my refrigerator because the spinach bag was taking up so much space, but all the while I told myself that the hassle was worth it. Yet, a week later, I would have to throw away half of the bag of spinach because it was going bad. Finally, I realized it made much more sense to just buy a smaller bag of spinach, even if the price per pound was more.

Prepare certain pantry items in bulk and store in the freezer. For example, I make a lot of pesto when basil is in season (and inexpensive) and freeze the pesto in ice cube trays. I pop the pesto cubes into a resealable plastic bag so that I always have pesto on hand. I do the same with lemon juice and lime juice. I also freeze or can fresh fruit and vegetables when they are in season to be used later in the year.

Make extra! I always try to double recipes (especially casseroles) so that I have a store of ready-made, quality entrées in my freezer. I also make extra rice and pasta to freeze for later use.

# It Only Takes A Dish

**P**art of streamlining the cooking process is using the fewest number of utensils and pieces of cookware to create a fantastic meal. The recipes in this chapter only require one or two pieces of cookware, yet they still manage to produce layered, sophisticated flavors your family will love. These dishes are so scrumptious that you can even serve them during a special occasion or to guests. Better yet, you will have a minimum of cookware to wash after the meal, and in addition to our helper hints, you can always ask your child helpers to pitch in during cleanup!

By the end of this chapter, you will:

- create dishes that are quick, easy, and satisfying
- use one or two pieces of cookware to produce each dish
- learn which prepared items to take advantage of at your grocery store
- discover which alternate cuts of meat can be used to minimize cooking time
- learn which recipes can be prepared in advance
- entertain and educate your child helpers with fun food facts
- delegate certain food preparation tasks to your child helpers
- streamline your grocery shopping with our handy lists
- utilize your well-stocked pantry
- add tasty recipes to your repertoire of quick cooking, including layered skillets, stir-fries, and ragouts

# Layered Penne Pasta Bake

| | |
|---|---|
| 12 oz. | penne pasta, cooked and drained |
| 1 lb. | ground beef or sausage |
| 1 c. | onion, chopped |
| 1 clove | garlic, minced |
| 1 15-oz. | can Italian style tomato sauce |
| 1 14-1/2 oz. | can diced tomatoes with herbs |
| 1 6-oz. can | tomato paste |
| 1/2 c. | water |
| 4 c. | shredded mozzarella cheese |

Preheat the oven to 325°F. Brown the meat, onion and the garlic in a skillet. Pour off any excess fat. Add the tomato sauce, undrained tomatoes, tomato paste and the water. Cook, stirring occasionally, for 10 minutes. Layer half of the cooked pasta, half of the sauce, and half of the cheese in a 9" x 13" baking pan. Repeat the layers. Cover and bake for 15 minutes until the casserole is bubbling and cooked through. Makes 8 servings.

Kids can help with this recipe:

1. Measure the water and shredded cheese.
2. Older kids, with instruction, can open the canned tomato products with a can opener.

**Teachable Moment:** Kids might be interested to learn that penne pasta is actually a larger version of macaroni cut on the diagonal. It has been claimed that Marco Polo brought pasta to Italy on his return from China, but historians know that pasta existed independently in both cultures prior to Polo's adventures.

## quick tip

Plan ahead for those moments when you're scrambling to have dinner on the table. Double this recipe and make two casseroles instead of one. Before baking, freeze one to be used up to three months later. When needed, you can just pop the extra frozen casserole into the oven and heat at 350°F for 1 hour or until heated through. Add crusty Italian bread and a crisp green salad to round out this delicious, fuss-free meal.

## Your Shopping List:

- ❏ 1 12-oz. box of penne pasta
- ❏ 1 lb. ground beef or sausage
- ❏ 1 small yellow or white onion
- ❏ 1 15-oz. can of tomato sauce
- ❏ 1 14-1/2 oz. can of diced tomatoes with Italian herbs
- ❏ 1 6-oz. can of tomato paste or tubed tomato paste

### From Your Pantry:
- ❏ garlic

## Beef & Root Vegetable Ragout

| | |
|---|---|
| 4 T. | extra-virgin olive oil |
| 1 medium | yellow onion, chopped |
| 1 clove | garlic, minced |
| 1-1/2 lb. | beef stew meat, cut into 1-inch cubes |
| 4 T. | red wine vinegar |
| 1 c. | beef broth |
| 1 | bay leaf |
| 1/2 t. | dried oregano |
| 1/2 c. | tomato sauce |
| 1/2 t. | salt |
| 1/4 t. | freshly ground black pepper |
| 1 T. | fresh basil, chopped |
| 4 | baking potatoes, peeled and cubed |
| 2 | carrots, peeled and sliced |

In a large stockpot over medium-high heat, heat the oil and sauté the onions and garlic until the onions are translucent. Add the meat and sear on all sides. Reduce the heat to medium and add the vinegar, broth, bay leaf, oregano, tomato sauce, salt, and black pepper. Reduce the heat to low, cover the stockpot, and simmer for 1 hour. Add the fresh basil, potatoes, and carrots and simmer for an additional 30 minutes or until the vegetables are fork-tender. To serve, remove the bay leaf and ladle the ragout into large dinner bowls. Makes 4 servings.

Kids can help with this recipe:

1.  Measure the liquids: red wine vinegar and beef broth.
2.  Measure the dry seasonings: oregano, salt, and pepper.
3.  Older kids, with instruction, are able to open the can of tomato sauce with a can opener.
4.  Wash the potatoes and carrots with water and a vegetable scrubber.

**Teachable Moment:** Root vegetables such as potatoes and carrots grow underground and provide nourishment to the growing plant above. Once they have grown to a certain size, farmers harvest them. Explain to your child helper that because these vegetables, also known as tubers, have grown in the dirt, they need to be washed and scrubbed very well. Other root vegetables include beets, parsnips, turnips, and lotus.

## Your Shopping List:

1 medium yellow onion
1-1/2 lbs. beef stew meat
1 14-1/2 oz. can of beef broth
1 15-oz. can of tomato sauce
1 bunch of fresh basil
4 medium baking potatoes
2 medium carrots

### From Your Pantry:

extra-virgin olive oil, garlic, red wine vinegar, bay leaf, dried oregano, salt, pepper

## quick tip

Instead of using full-scale carrots, you can utilize an equivalent amount of peeled, bagged baby carrots (the kind that you snack on) so there's no peeling and slicing. Likewise, cube red jacket potatoes or new potatoes and don't bother with the time-consuming task of peeling potato skins. The ragout will be equally tasty.

# Pan-Pacific Stir-Fry Beef

| | |
|---|---|
| 1-1/2 lbs. | beef round steak (partially frozen) |
| 1/4 c. | vegetable oil |
| 1 small | onion, sliced |
| 1-1/2 c. | celery, cut in thin diagonal slices |
| 1 c. | carrots, cut in thin diagonal slices |
| 1 T. | cornstarch |
| 1/4 c. | soy sauce |
| 1 8 oz. | can tomato sauce |
| 1 t. | sugar |
| 1/4 t. | ginger |
| 1/2 | green bell pepper, cut in strips |
| 1/2 | yellow bell pepper, cut in strips |
| 1/2 c. | fresh mushrooms, thinly sliced |
| 1/2 c. | sliced water chestnuts |
| 6 c. | hot, cooked rice |

Cut the partially frozen steak into thin strips about 2 inches in length. Heat the oil in a large skillet or wok and cook the steak for 2 minutes over high heat. Add the onion, celery and carrots and cook until tender-crisp (about 4 minutes). In a small bowl, combine the cornstarch, soy sauce, tomato sauce, sugar, and ginger. Add the sauce to the skillet and heat through. Add the bell peppers, mushrooms, and water chestnuts. Cook and stir for 3 to 4 minutes, or until the sauce is thickened and the vegetables are heated. Serve over hot rice. Makes 4 servings.

## quick tip

Check your local supermarket for bagged, pre-cut Asian stir-fry vegetables. Often these vegetables are already washed, julienned, and ready to go. Depending on their vegetable content, you can substitute 3 cups of them for the onion, celery, and carrots. Similarly, take advantage of the convenience of pre-sliced, pre-washed white button or shiitake mushrooms available in most supermarkets.

Kids can help with this recipe:

1. Wash the carrots, celery, and green bell pepper.

2. Use a paper towel to clean the fresh, whole mushrooms.

3. Older kids, with instruction, will be able to open the cans of tomato sauce and water chestnuts with a can opener.

4. Measure the following ingredients and combine in a small bowl: cornstarch, soy sauce, tomato sauce, sugar, and ginger.

5. Set the minute timer while the steak and vegetables cook.

**Teachable Moment:** Let your child helper closely examine the fresh, unpeeled ginger, and explain that it is a root that has a tangy strong taste. Most ginger is grown in Jamaica, but it is also grown in India, China, and Africa. The root is used fresh in Chinese, Japanese, and East Indian cooking. Dried, powdered ginger is used in European baking, such as in gingerbread and gingersnap cookies.

# Your Shopping List:

1-1/2 lbs. round steak
1 small yellow onion*
2 stalks of celery*
2 medium carrots*
1 large green bell pepper
6 large, fresh mushrooms (or 1 package of sliced mushrooms)
4-oz. can of sliced water chestnuts
8-oz. can of tomato sauce
1 2-lb. bag of minute rice or jasmine rice

## From Your Pantry:

cornstarch, soy sauce, sugar, ground ginger

*(or 3 c. bagged, prepared Asian stir-fry vegetables)

# Tasty Tostada Skillet

| | |
|---|---|
| 1 16-oz. | can refried beans |
| 1/4 t. | ground cumin |
| 1 c. | cooked lean beef, cut into thin slices |
| 1/4 c. | prepared taco sauce |
| 1 c. | cheddar cheese, shredded |
| 1/4 c. | green onions, thinly sliced |
| 1 | tomato, chopped |
| 1 T. | fresh cilantro leaves |
| | salsa for garnish |
| 8 | prepared corn tostada shells |

Spread the refried beans in the bottom of a large skillet. Sprinkle with the ground cumin. Heat the beans over medium-low heat until warmed and slightly steaming, stirring occasionally. Spread the beans into an even layer and top with the beef. Pour the taco sauce over the beef. Sprinkle the cheddar cheese over the sauce. Cover and cook on medium heat for 5 to 6 minutes or until the cheese is melted and the tostada is cooked through. Layer the green onions over the cheese, spread the tomato evenly over the onions, and top with the cilantro. To serve, divide the skillet into fourths and scoop equal portions of the tostada filling onto the tostada shells. Garnish with salsa. Makes 4 servings.

Kids can help with this recipe:

1. Older kids, with instruction, can open the can of refried beans and place the beans into the skillet.
2. Measure the cumin and taco sauce.
3. Carefully sprinkle the shredded cheese over the meat layer.
4. Wash the green onions, tomato, and cilantro. Pick the cilantro leaves off the stems.
5. Open the box of tostada shells and place 2 on each dinner plate.

## quick tip

Instead of preparing the separate ingredients of green onions, tomato, and fresh cilantro, use prepared "pico de gallo" instead. Pico de gallo is a fresh, chopped, Mexican salsa that consists of tomato, onion, chilies, and cilantro. You can find pico de gallo in the refrigerated section of your supermarket. Spread a cup of the pico de gallo (drained of juice) over the melted cheese layer of the tostada for a quick finish to your cooking.

**Teachable Moment:** Tell your child-helper that a tostada is a crispy fried tortilla covered in your favorite toppings. Zapotec Indians of Mexico created the tostada as a way to preserve tortillas. Because it didn't spoil for many weeks, the Zapotecs could travel from place to place and bring tostadas with them. Because the tostada serves as an easy-to-hold, edible plate, it is one of the most popular street foods in present-day Mexico.

# Your Shopping List:

1 16-oz. can of refried beans
1 cup cooked lean beef, cut into thin slices
1 jar of prepared taco sauce
1 package of shredded cheddar cheese
1 bunch of green onions*
1 large tomato*
1 bunch of fresh cilantro*
1 jar of your favorite salsa*
1 box of prepared corn tostada shells (at least 8 in the box)

## From Your Pantry:

ground cumin

(*Or one refrigerated container of pico de gallo)

# Thai Basil Tenderloin Steak

| | |
|---|---|
| 2 T. | sesame oil |
| 2 cloves | garlic, minced |
| 2 | jalapeño or Thai bird chilies, seeded and minced |
| 1 lb. | beef tenderloin, thinly sliced |
| 1-1/2 T. | Southeast Asian fish sauce |
| 1 t. | brown sugar |
| 1 T. | fresh Italian basil or Thai basil leaves, finely minced |
| 2 T. | salted peanuts, chopped |

In a large wok or deep skillet, sauté the garlic and chilies in the oil for 1 minute. Add the beef slices and cook for 2 minutes on medium-heat, stirring constantly. In a small bowl, combine the fish sauce, sugar, and basil and pour over the beef slices. Cook and stir for 2 minutes. Serve over Thai rice noodles or jasmine rice. Garnish with fresh basil and chopped peanuts. Makes 4 servings.

Kids can assist you with this recipe:

1. Measure the sesame oil, fish sauce, brown sugar, and salted peanuts
2. Wash the basil
3. Separate the basil leaves from their stems.

**Teachable Moment:** Fish sauce is used as a condiment throughout Southeast Asia. It is made from the liquid of salted, fermented fish.

## Your Shopping List:

2 jalapeño or Thai bird chilies
1 lb. beef tenderloin
1 bunch of fresh basil (Italian or Thai)
1 6-1/2 oz. bag of chopped peanuts
(found with ice cream topping items)
Thai rice noodles or jasmine rice

### From Your Pantry:

sesame oil, garlic, fish sauce, brown sugar

## quick tip

Place the beef in the freezer for 20 minutes before slicing. Doing so will allow you to carve extremely thin slices that cook very quickly. You can prepare this meal a day in advance as it is equally delicious served cool over a bed of cold rice noodles or warm rice. Jazz it up with julienned carrots and cucumber for a well-balanced meal.

# Pesto & Three Cheese Pizza

Use homemade pizza dough or prepackaged pizza rounds.

**Pesto:**

| | |
|---|---|
| 1 c. | extra-virgin olive oil |
| 2 c. | fresh basil leaves |
| 2 cloves | garlic, minced |
| 3 T. | pine nuts |
| 1/2 c. | Parmesan cheese, grated |

Into a blender, combine the olive oil, basil, garlic, and the pine nuts. Process until almost pureed. Stir in the cheese and set aside.

**Toppings:**

| | |
|---|---|
| 1 | onion, thinly sliced |
| 1 | sweet red pepper, sliced |
| 1 | green pepper, sliced |
| 2 T. | extra-virgin olive oil |
| 1 T. | water |
| 1/2 lb. | garlic sausage |
| 1/2 lb. | sweet Italian sausage |
| 2 T. | cornmeal |
| 1/4 c. | goat cheese |
| 3/4 c. | mozzarella cheese, shredded |
| 2 T. | Parmesan cheese, grated |

Sauté the onions and peppers over medium heat in 1 tablespoon of the olive oil and the water. When the peppers are soft, drain and set aside. Brown the sausage and drain off the excess fat. Coarsely chop the sausage. Preheat the oven to 400°F.

Spread the remaining oil over a 12-inch pizza pan and sprinkle the cornmeal over the oil. Place the pizza dough on the pan and flatten to the edges. Spread the pesto on the dough and then crumble the goat cheese evenly over the pesto. Add the onion, peppers, sausage, and the remaining cheeses. Bake 15 minutes or until the crust is slightly brown and the cheese is bubbly. Makes 4 servings.

Kids can help with this recipe:

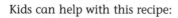

1. Wash the basil and remove the leaves from the stems.

2. Spread the pesto on the pizza dough with a pastry brush.

3. Put the toppings on the pizza.

**Teachable Moment:** Kids will be interested in learning that pizza is a Mediterranean invention that was made famous in Italy. The first pizza sold in America was made by a 13-year-old in the Little Italy neighborhood of New York City.

# Your Shopping List:

1 bunch of fresh basil*
1 bag of pine nuts*
1 container of freshly grated Parmesan cheese*
1 small red onion
1 sweet red pepper
1 green bell pepper
1/2 lb. garlic sausage
1/2 lb. sweet Italian sausage
1/4 c. goat cheese
1 8-oz. bag of shredded mozzarella cheese
pizza dough or prepared pizza rounds

# From Your Pantry:

cornmeal, extra-virgin olive oil, garlic

(*or 1 jar of prepared pesto)

## quick tip

Instead of making the pesto, you can buy prepared pesto. Fresh, prepared pesto can be found in the refrigerated section of the supermarket, or you can also find sealed jars of pesto in the Italian sauce aisle.

# Citrus Soy Tuna

| 4 6-oz. | fresh tuna steaks, about 1 inch thick |
| 1/4 c. | soy sauce |
| 1/4 c. | mandarin juice |
| 3 strips | mandarin zest |
| 3 T. | clover honey |
| dash | hot pepper sauce |
| 1 T. | fresh cilantro, chopped |

Combine the soy sauce, mandarin juice, mandarin zest, honey, hot pepper sauce, and the fresh cilantro and shake in a sealed, resealable plastic bag until blended. Add the tuna steaks and coat each side with the marinade. Seal and place the steaks in the refrigerator to marinate for 30 to 60 minutes, turning the bag once.

Preheat the grill to high. With a slotted spatula, remove the tuna steaks from the marinade. Strain the marinade into a small saucepan and boil to a thick, syrupy glaze. Grill the fish until cooked to taste, 4 to 6 minutes per side for medium. Brush the tuna steaks with the glaze as they grill. Serve immediately. Makes 4 servings.

Kids can assist you with this recipe:

1. Measure the soy sauce, mandarin juice, and honey.
2. Place the ingredients in the resealable bag.

**Teachable Moment:** Bees make honey as food storage for the months in which fresh nectar is unavailable to them. The color and flavor of honey depends on the type of blossoms the honeybees visit. Honeybees have to visit over 1 million flowers to produce 1 pound of honey! Amazing!

# Your Shopping List:

4 6-oz. fresh tuna steaks, about 1 inch thick
1 pint of mandarin juice
1 mandarin, for its zest
1 bunch of fresh cilantro

## From Your Pantry:

soy sauce, honey, hot pepper sauce, gallon-size resealable bag

# quick tip

Preplan for those hectic evenings when dinner seems impossible. Double the recipe and place four of the tuna steaks with half the sauce into a freezer bag. Remove as much air as possible from the bag. Place in the freezer for up to two months before using. Just remember to put the tuna steaks in the refrigerator to thaw overnight before grilling.

# Grilled Pork Tenderloin with Tomato-Basil Concasse

| 2 lbs. | pork tenderloin |
| | salt and ground black pepper to taste |

**Glaze and Dressing:**

| 3 T. | extra-virgin olive oil |
| 3 T. | red wine vinegar |
| 1/2 t. | salt |
| 1/2 t. | sugar |
| 1/4 t. | ground black pepper |
| 1/2 t. | dried thyme |

**Tomato-Basil Concasse:**

| 3 c. | cherry and grape tomatoes, both red and yellow, washed and quartered |
| 1/2 medium | red onion, peeled and finely chopped |
| 1/2 c. | fresh basil leaves, minced |

Rub the pork with salt and pepper to taste and set aside.

In a small bowl, whisk together the olive oil, vinegar, salt, sugar, pepper, and thyme until thoroughly combined. Reserve 1 tablespoon of the dressing to use as a glaze over the pork. Cover and refrigerate the remaining dressing.

Preheat the grill to medium-high heat. Sear the meat quickly on all sides on the grill for 2 to 3 minutes. Reduce the grill heat to medium. Brush 1 tablespoon of glaze on all sides of the tenderloin. Grill for 30 to 45 minutes, rotating the tenderloin every 7 to 10 minutes. The meat is done when a meat thermometer reaches an internal temperature of 160°F. Remove the meat from the grill, place it on a cutting board, cover it with foil, and let it rest for 10 minutes.

In a medium bowl, combine the tomatoes, onions, and the basil. Stir in the chilled olive oil dressing and mix well. To serve, slice the tenderloin diagonally and top with the tomato relish. Makes 4 servings.

## quick tip

If you're really pressed for time, grill four bone-in pork chops instead of the pork tenderloin to reduce cooking time. Make sure the pork chops are about 3/4-inch thick. As with the tenderloin, season the chops with salt and pepper to taste. Grill each chop for 4 to 5 minutes per side or until cooked through. Top with the tomato-basil concasse for a quick and colorful entrée.

Kids can help with this recipe:

1. Rub the pork tenderloin with salt and pepper. (Remember to wash your hands with soap and warm water afterwards!)

2. Measure and whisk together the extra-virgin olive oil, red wine vinegar, salt, sugar, ground black pepper, and dried thyme for the dressing and glaze.

3. Wash and dry the cherry and grape tomatoes. (Older kids, with supervision and a child-safe paring knife, can quarter the tomatoes.)

4. Separate the basil leaves from the stems. Wash and dry the leaves.

**Teachable Moment:** You can tell your child helper that basil symbolizes love in Italy. It is a popular herb with varieties in many colors. There's even cinnamon basil and lemon basil that smell like their namesakes. The herb is one of the few that grows stronger in flavor when cooked.

# Your Shopping List:

2 lbs. pork tenderloin
3 c. cherry and grape tomatoes, both red and yellow
1 medium red onion
1 bunch of fresh basil

## From Your Pantry:

salt, ground black pepper, extra-virgin olive oil, red wine vinegar, sugar, dried thyme

# Pork Medallions with Pasta Ribbons

| | |
|---|---|
| 1 lb. | pork tenderloin, cut into 8 medallions |
| 1 T. | butter |
| 1 c. | fresh white mushrooms, sliced |
| 2 T. | white onion, finely chopped |
| 1/4 t. | celery salt |
| 1/4 t. | ground black pepper |
| 1 clove | garlic, minced |
| 8 oz. | wide egg noodles, cooked al dente and drained |

Press each slice of tenderloin to a 1-inch thickness. In a large skillet, melt the butter over medium-high heat. Sear the pork medallions quickly (about 1 minute on each side). Remove the pork from the pan and keep warm. To the drippings in the skillet, add the mushrooms, onion, celery salt, black pepper, and garlic. Cook and stir over low heat for 2 minutes. Cover and simmer for 3 to 4 minutes. To serve, place equal portions of noodles on four individual plates. Top each plate with two pork medallions and cover with the mushroom sauce.  Makes 4 servings.

Kids can help with this recipe:

1. Clean the mushrooms with a paper towel or damp towel.
2. Fill a pot with water for cooking the pasta.
3. Measure the sliced mushrooms, onion, celery salt, and black pepper and add to the skillet.
4. Mince the garlic in a garlic press and add to the skillet.

# Your Shopping List:

1 lb. pork tenderloin
1 c. fresh white mushrooms
1 small white onion
8 oz. wide egg noodles

## From Your Pantry:

butter, celery salt, ground black pepper, garlic

## quick tip

Your supermarket butcher is your quick-cook friend! He or she will gladly slice the pork tenderloin into medallions for you to save you from that additional step. In addition, you can buy a package of pre-cleaned, pre-sliced white mushrooms in the produce section of the market.

# Arroz Español

| | |
|---|---|
| 4 c. | hot, cooked long grain white rice |
| 1 16-oz. | can tomato sauce |
| 1/2 small | white onion, finely chopped |
| 1 | green bell pepper, finely chopped |
| 3 | mild Italian sausages, cooked |
| 1 t. | ground chili powder |
| 1/2 t. | salt |

Combine the rice, tomato sauce, onion and green pepper in a mixing bowl and blend well. Cut the sausage into small pieces and add to the rice and vegetables. Sprinkle the rice with the chili powder and salt and mix again. Coat a large baking pan with cooking spray and spread the rice in the pan, smoothing the top evenly. Bake at 350°F for 15 minutes or until it is hot throughout. Makes 4 servings.

Kids can help with this recipe:

1. Clean and deseed the bell pepper.
2. Older kids can, with supervision, open the can of tomato sauce with a can opener.
3. Measure the ground chili powder and salt.
4. Coat the large baking pan with cooking spray.

# Your Shopping List:

2 c. long grain white rice
1 16-oz. can of tomato sauce
1 small white onion
1 green bell pepper
3 mild Italian sausages

## From Your Pantry:

ground chili powder, salt, cooking spray

## quick tip

Use quick-cooking long grain rice to speed up the preparation of the rice. (There are even microwaveable products that cook rice in just 90 seconds!) You can also use ground, mild Italian sausage filling (available in the meat section of your grocery store) and cook the filling as you would ground beef. Add the cooked, ground filling to the rice instead of the sausage pieces for added flavor.

# Cheddar Pasta with Ham and Broccoli

| | |
|---|---|
| 2 c. | fully cooked ham, chopped |
| 3 c. | macaroni pasta, cooked and drained |
| 1 c. | fresh broccoli, cut into small florets |
| 1/2 c. | cheddar cheese, shredded |
| 3 | green onions, thinly sliced |
| 1 10-3/4 oz. | can condensed cheddar cheese soup |
| 1/4 c. | milk |
| 1/2 t. | black pepper |
| 3/4 c. | Asiago cheese, grated |

Lightly coat a 2-quart baking dish with cooking spray. In a large bowl, combine the ham, pasta, broccoli, cheddar cheese, and green onions. Blend the soup and milk in a small bowl and add to the ham and vegetables. Transfer the contents to the baking dish. Sprinkle with black pepper and top with the Asiago cheese. Cover and bake at 350°F for 30 minutes. Uncover and bake for 10 minutes. Makes 6 servings.

Kids can help with this recipe:

1. Coat the baking dish with cooking spray.

2. Fill a stockpot with water to cook the macaroni pasta.

3. Wash the broccoli and green onions.

4. With supervision, older kids can open the can of cheddar cheese soup with a can opener.

5. Mix the ham, pasta, broccoli, cheddar cheese, and green onions in the mixing bowl.

6. Whisk together the soup and milk and add to the mixing bowl with the previous ingredients.

7. Measure and sprinkle the ground pepper and asiago cheese on top of the baking dish contents.

## quick tip

Take advantage of your grocery store's offering of pre-washed, pre-cut vegetables. Instead of a head of broccoli, buy a bag of broccoli florets. For variation, you could also use a mixed bag of broccoli and cauliflower florets. Likewise, buy the pre-shredded cheddar cheese and Asiago cheese to make your life a little bit easier.

**Teachable Moment:** Asiago cheese is made from cow's milk and has a rich, nutty flavor. Cheese-makers form it into small rounds and it is kept in a cool, dark place to age for over a year.

# Your Shopping List:

2 c. fully cooked ham
3 c. macaroni pasta
1 head of fresh broccoli (or 1 bag of broccoli florets)
1 small bag of shredded cheddar cheese
1 bunch of green onions
1 10-3/4 oz. can of condensed cheddar cheese soup
1 small container of shredded asiago cheese

# From Your Pantry:

milk, black pepper, cooking spray

# Pasta alla Carbonara

| | |
|---|---|
| 10 c. | water |
| 1 t. | salt |
| 1 lb. | spaghetti, broken in half |
| 1/4 lb. | pancetta (you may use 1/4 lb. American bacon, if desired) |
| 2 | eggs, beaten |
| 1 c. | frozen peas, thawed |
| | salt and pepper to taste |
| 1/4 c. | freshly grated Parmesan cheese |
| 1 T. | Italian flat-leaf parsley, minced |

In a large stockpot, heat the water to a boil and add the salt. Cook the spaghetti noodles in the boiling water until they are al dente. Reserve some of the pasta cooking water. Drain the pasta and set aside.

While the pasta is cooking, cut the pancetta into small cubes and fry over medium-high heat in a large sauté pan until well-browned (about 4 minutes). Add the hot, drained pasta and peas to the sauté pan. Combine the beaten eggs and Parmesan cheese in a small bowl and add to the hot pasta. Working quickly, remove from the heat and toss to combine. Add some of the reserved pasta water if more liquid is needed for a smooth sauce. Season with salt and pepper to taste. Toss again. Garnish with a sprinkling of parsley. Serve immediately. Makes 4 servings.

Kids can help with this recipe:

1. Measure the water and place in the stockpot.
2. Crack open the eggs and beat with a fork.
3. Measure the frozen peas and Parmesan cheese.
4. Wash the flat-leaf parsley.

**Teachable Moment:** This is a great opportunity to explain to your child helper about the importance of cooking pasta correctly. There needs to be plenty of water for boiling the pasta, and the water needs to be salted to enhance the pasta's flavor. The pasta is done when it is "al dente" – meaning "to the tooth." It will not be hard, but it will also not be too soft and mushy.

# Your Shopping List:

1/4 lb. pancetta (or 1/4 lb. American bacon, if desired)
1 lb. spaghetti
2 eggs
1 8-oz. pkg. frozen peas
1/4 c. Parmesan cheese, grated

## From Your Pantry:

salt, ground black pepper

## quick tip

The refrigerated cheese section of most grocery stores now carries tubs of freshly grated hard cheeses, such as Parmesan. These tubs are more flavorful than the grated Parmesan cheese that is stored on the shelf but just as convenient.

# Prosciutto & Peas in Angel Hair Pasta

| 1/2 lb. | prosciutto, diced |
| 1-1/2 c. | frozen peas, thawed |
| 1-1/2 c. | prepared Alfredo sauce |
| 1 t. | freshly ground black pepper |
| 8 oz. | angel hair pasta, cooked al dente and drained |

In a medium saucepan, lightly sauté the prosciutto for 3 minutes. In the same saucepan, add the peas, Alfredo sauce, and pepper. Cook over medium-low heat until the sauce is smooth and heated through. Ladle the sauce over the pasta onto individual plates. Makes 4 servings.

Kids can help with this recipe:

1. Fill a stockpot with water for cooking the pasta.
2. Measure the frozen peas.
3. Open the container of Alfredo sauce and measure.
4. Measure the black pepper.

**Teachable Moment:** Angel hair pasta is so named because the long, thin strands look like the hairs of an angel. It is also called capellini, which means "hair" in Italian.

# Your Shopping List:

1/2 lb. prosciutto, diced
1 package of frozen peas
1 container of prepared Alfredo sauce
1 package of angel hair pasta or capellini

## From Your Pantry:
ground black pepper

## quick tip

Angel hair (also known as capellini) is the perfect pasta for a quick meal. It takes only a few minutes to cook and is versatile and elegant.

The convenience of prepared Alfredo sauce cannot be beat. However, there is a wide range of quality and taste with these sauces. In general, the refrigerated sauces (in clear tubs) are tastier than the jarred varieties. Look for an Alfredo sauce that is full of wholesome ingredients and has a minimum of preservatives.

# Layered Turkey Taco Salad

| | |
|---|---|
| 1 lb. | ground turkey |
| 1/2 c. | yellow onion, chopped |
| 1/2 c. | green bell pepper, chopped |
| 1 clove | garlic, minced |
| 1 1-oz. | pkg. taco seasoning mix |
| 1 c. | tortilla chips, crushed |
| 1 c. | cheddar cheese, shredded |
| 2 c. | iceberg lettuce, shredded |
| 1 c. | garden tomato, diced |
| 1 8-oz. | can sliced black olives, drained |
| 1 c. | dairy sour cream |
| | hot pepper sauce, to taste |

Preheat an oven to 375°F. Spray a 2 qt. baking pan with cooking spray. In a skillet, brown the ground turkey, onions, peppers, and the garlic. Add the seasoning mix to the meat, cooking as directed by the seasoning mix instructions. Place half of the crushed chips in the bottom of the baking pan. Add all of the meat mixture to cover the chips. Sprinkle with the cheddar cheese and top with the remaining crushed chips. Bake uncovered for 30 minutes. Remove from the oven and top with lettuce, tomato, sour cream, and sliced black olives. Serve with hot pepper sauce on the side. Makes 8 servings.

Kids can help with this recipe:

1. Clean and deseed the green bell pepper.
2. Mince the garlic clove in a garlic press.
3. Measure and crush the tortilla chips.
4. Measure the cheddar cheese and dairy sour cream.
5. Older kids can, with supervision, open the can of black olives with a can opener and then drain.
6. Apply cooking spray to the baking pan.
7. Sprinkle the cheddar cheese on the dish before placing it in the oven.
8. Carefully top the dish with the lettuce, tomato, sour cream, and sliced black olives without touching the hot baking pan.

# Your Shopping List:

1 lb. ground turkey
1 small yellow onion
1 green bell pepper
1 1-oz. package of taco seasoning mix
1/2 c. prepared salsa
1 container of dairy sour cream
1 bag of tortilla chips*
1 small package of shredded cheddar cheese
1 small head of iceberg lettuce
2 medium-ripe garden tomatoes
1 8-oz. can of sliced black olives

## From Your Pantry:

garlic, cooking spray, hot pepper sauce

(*or 1 package of 10 flour tortillas)

## quick tip

If 30 minutes in the oven is too long for you to wait, you can also assemble these ingredients without the tortilla chips and make burritos. Just buy a package of flour tortillas with enough for each person. You can heat up the tortillas on a greaseless griddle on the stovetop or pop them in the microwave. Each family member can choose the ingredients for their burritos and make their own. Voilá…instant Tex-Mex feast!

# Papaya Glazed Chicken

| | |
|---|---|
| 1 8 oz. | can tomato sauce |
| 1/2 c. | orange juice |
| 1/2 c. | white onion, finely chopped |
| 1 T. | jalapeño peppers, diced |
| 1/2 t. | dried oregano |
| 1/2 t. | chili powder |
| 1/4 t. | ground cumin |
| 1 clove | garlic, minced |
| 1 T. | fresh cilantro, chopped |
| 2 dashes | hot pepper sauce |
| 5 | chicken breast halves, boneless, skinless, cut into 1-inch pieces |
| 2 t. | cornstarch |
| 1 T. | chicken broth |
| 1 c. | fresh papaya, chopped |
| 3 c. | hot cooked rice |
| 1 T. | fresh cilantro, chopped, as garnish |

In a large skillet over medium heat, combine the tomato sauce, orange juice, onion, jalapeños, oregano, chili powder, cumin, garlic, cilantro, and hot pepper sauce. Bring to a boil, stirring occasionally as the ingredients heat. Reduce the heat to low, cover, and simmer for 5 minutes.

Add the chicken pieces to the skillet and bring the sauce back to boiling. Cover and simmer for 12 to 15 minutes, until the chicken is tender and no longer pink. In a small bowl, stir together the cornstarch and the chicken broth until smooth. Stir into the skillet and cook until thickened and bubbly. Stir and cook 2 additional minutes. Add the papaya and cook just until the papaya is warm. To serve, place the hot rice on a warm platter and cover with the chicken and papaya sauce. Sprinkle with fresh cilantro. Makes 6 servings.

Kids can help with this recipe:

1. Measure the orange juice, oregano, chili powder, cumin, and hot pepper sauce and place in the skillet.

2. Older kids, with supervision, can open the tomato sauce can with a can opener and place the sauce in the skillet.

## quick tip

When you're on the go, every minute counts. If you use a lot of garlic in your cooking, buy the minced garlic in a jar available at supermarkets. It will save you the step of peeling the garlic and mincing it, and your hands will not take on that garlic odor!

3. Wash the cilantro.

4. Measure and stir together the cornstarch and chicken broth.

5. Scoop out the papaya seeds.

6. Sprinkle the fresh cilantro garnish over the finished dish.

**Teachable Moment:** Teach your child helper about papayas. They are a popular, tropical fruit native to North America. When ripe, they are large and pear-shaped, with a bright yellow skin. Most papayas grown in the United States are from Hawaii or Florida. Papayas are also grown in many tropical regions throughout the world.

# Your Shopping List:

1 8-oz. can of tomato sauce
1 pint orange juice
1 medium white onion
1 jalapeño pepper
1 bunch of fresh cilantro
5 boneless, skinless chicken breast halves
1 fresh papaya

## From Your Pantry:

dried oregano, chili powder, ground cumin, garlic, hot pepper sauce, cornstarch, chicken broth

# Ginger Chicken Citron

| | |
|---|---|
| 3 to 3-1/2 lbs. | roasting chicken, cut into individual pieces |
| 2 T. | butter |
| 1 t. | salt |
| 1/8 t. | ground ginger |
| 1/8 t. | ground black pepper |
| 1 t. | fresh ginger, minced |
| 3 | carrots, peeled and cut julienne |
| 1 small | white onion, thinly sliced |
| 2/3 c. | fresh orange juice |
| 1 T. | cornstarch |
| 1/3 c. | orange marmalade |
| 3 T. | dark brown sugar |
| 1 T. | lemon juice |
| 1/4 t. | hot pepper sauce |
| 2 | green onions, thinly sliced, for garnish (optional) |

In a large skillet over medium heat, melt the butter and brown the chicken pieces. Combine the salt, ground ginger, and pepper in a small bowl and sprinkle over the chicken. Add the fresh ginger, carrots, and onions to the skillet. In a medium bowl, combine the orange juice and the cornstarch, stirring until smooth. Add the orange marmalade, brown sugar, lemon juice, and the hot pepper sauce and stir well. Pour the orange juice mixture over the chicken and vegetables. Bring to a boil. Reduce the heat, cover, and simmer 45 to 50 minutes until a meat thermometer registers 170°F when inserted to the thickest part of the chicken thigh and no pink remains. Sprinkle sliced green onions over each serving. Makes 4 to 6 servings.

## quick tip

This is a recipe where all the component parts can be prepared the night before, allowing the dish to be thrown together at the last moment. Place the seasoned chicken pieces in a large resealable bag. Prepare the vegetables and fresh ginger and place in a resealable plastic bag. Prepare the orange juice mixture and keep in a sealed plastic container. Keep all of these containers in the refrigerator. When you come home from your busy day, just assemble and cook!

Kids can help with this recipe:

1. Measure the butter and place in the skillet to be melted.
2. Wash and peel the carrots with a child-safe vegetable peeler.
3. Measure the orange juice and cornstarch, mixing until smooth.

4. Squeeze the lemon for lemon juice.

5. Measure the orange marmalade, brown sugar, lemon juice, and hot pepper sauce, and add to the orange juice mixture.

6. Pour the final orange juice mixture over the chicken in the skillet with supervision.

7. Sprinkle the green onions, as garnish, over the finished dish.

# Your Shopping List:

3 to 3-1/2 lbs. roasting chicken, cut into individual pieces
3 medium carrots
1 small white onion
1 small piece of fresh ginger
1 pint fresh orange juice
1 small jar of orange marmalade
1 lemon
1 bunch of green onions (optional)

## From Your Pantry:

butter, salt, ground ginger, ground black pepper, cornstarch, dark brown sugar, hot pepper sauce

# Pepperoni Pizza Sticks

| | |
|---|---|
| 1 11-oz. | can soft bread sticks |
| 24 | pepperoni pieces, thinly sliced |
| 2 T. | Parmesan cheese, grated |
| 1/2 t. | dried Italian seasoning |
| 1/4 t. | garlic powder |
| 1/2 c. | prepared pizza sauce, heated |

Preheat the oven to 350°F. Unroll the bread sticks on a lightly floured surface. Place three pepperoni slices in a single layer over one half of each bread stick. Fold the remaining half of the bread stick over the top of the pepperoni. Seal the end of the bread stick and twist. Place the bread sticks on an ungreased baking sheet. Combine the Parmesan cheese, Italian seasoning, and the garlic powder. Sprinkle this mixture evenly over each bread stick. Bake for 15 to 20 minutes, until golden brown. Serve the pizza sticks accompanied by the heated pizza sauce. Makes 8 pizza sticks.

Kids can help with this recipe:

1. Place the pepperoni slices over the bread stick.
2. Fold the bread stick over the layer of pepperoni.
3. Place the bread sticks on an ungreased baking sheet.
4. Measure and combine the Parmesan cheese, Italian seasoning, and garlic powder.

# Your Shopping List:

1 11-oz. can of soft bread sticks
1 bag of pepperoni pieces (at least 24), thinly sliced
1 container of freshly grated Parmesan cheese
1 small container of prepared pizza sauce

## From Your Pantry:

dried Italian seasoning, garlic powder

**quick tip**

Rather than buying prepared pizza sauce, you can use leftover homemade or store-bought marinara sauce.

# Smoked Turkey and Gruyère Rolls

| | |
|---|---|
| 1 8-oz. | package refrigerated crescent rolls |
| 3 T. | prepared ranch salad dressing |
| 1/2 lb. | deli-style smoked turkey, sliced thinly |
| 8 | thin slices Gruyère cheese, about 2" x 4" |

Place the crescent rolls on a large baking sheet. Preheat the oven to 375°F. Spread the ranch dressing on the rolls and top each with smoked turkey slices. Layer the cheese on top of the turkey and roll each crescent, starting with the widest side of the roll and continuing to the narrow side. Bake for 25 to 30 minutes or until browned. Makes 8 servings.

Kids can help with this recipe:

1. Place the rolls on a large baking sheet.
2. Spread the ranch dressing on the rolls.
3. Layer cheese and turkey on each roll.
4. With supervision, roll each crescent.

**Teachable Moment:** Gruyère is a Swiss cheese with a sweet, nutty flavor and pale yellow interior. It is made into 100-pound wheels and aged for 10 to 12 months.

# Your Shopping List:

1 8-oz. package of refrigerated crescent rolls
1/2 lb. deli-style smoked turkey
8 thin slices of Gruyère cheese,
about 2" x 4"

## From Your Pantry:

prepared ranch salad dressing

## quick tip

In place of prepared crescent roll dough, you can use leftover croissants, bagels, or rolls and achieve the same effect. Just split each in half, layer with the ranch dressing, turkey, and cheese, and bake in the oven until the cheese is melted. You can also layer sliced tomato and fresh basil leaves for added flavor.

# It Only Takes A Minute

As any busy working parent will tell you, time is always of the essence. With our overscheduled lives, we might only have a short window of time between obligations to get dinner on the table. This chapter provides you with recipes that literally take only minutes yet deliver fantastic flavor. Additionally, these dishes are also very kid-friendly and appeal to their sense of taste and fun. Kids especially love the *Pepperoni Pizza Bagels* and *Crab and Cheese Muffin Melts.* All of the recipes provide opportunities for lots of parent-child involvement and interaction. So, instead relying on the fatty fast food kids' meals, you can use this chapter to provide your family with child-friendly home-cooking in just minutes!

By the end of this chapter, you will:

- create delicious dishes that only take minutes

- learn which supermarket shortcuts add flavor and cut time

- discover which recipe components can be made in advance

- learn that an easy resource for fresh pizza dough is your local pizzeria!

- understand why fresh pasta and couscous are a quick-cook's friends

- teach your child helper some fascinating food history

- make grocery shopping so much easier with our helpful lists

- understand the importance of a comprehensive pantry

- add amazing, tasty recipes to your dinner-time arsenal

# Huevos Rancheros

| | |
|---|---|
| 1 8-oz. | can tomato sauce |
| 1 t. | chili powder |
| 1/4 t. | cumin |
| 8 | eggs |
| 1/4 t. | black pepper |
| 1/8 t. | cayenne pepper |
| 1 c. | cheddar cheese, shredded |
| 4 | prepared tostada shells |

Preheat the oven to 350°F. In a lightly greased 9-inch pie pan, combine the tomato sauce, chili powder, and the cumin. Break the eggs evenly over the sauce in the dish. Sprinkle the eggs with the pepper and the paprika. Cover the pie pan with aluminum foil and bake for 15 to 20 minutes. Remove the aluminum foil, sprinkle the cheddar cheese over the eggs, and bake an additional 5 minutes. To serve, spoon two eggs, with sauce, into a tostada shell or tortilla, and garnish as you wish. Makes 4 servings.

Kids can help with this recipe:

1. Older kids, with supervision, can open the can of tomato sauce with a can opener.
2. Apply cooking spray to the pie pan.
3. Measure and combine the chili powder, cumin, and tomato sauce.
4. Older kids can break the eggs evenly over the sauce.
5. Sprinkle the eggs with black pepper and cayenne pepper.
6. Sprinkle the cheddar cheese over the eggs, carefully avoiding the hot pie pan.
7. Place the tostada shells on serving plates.

**Teachable Moment:** Huevos Rancheros is Spanish for "Ranch-Style Eggs" and is a specialty of the Sonoran region of Mexico. It is popular for breakfast, lunch, or dinner.

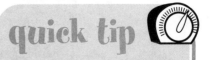

## quick tip

Instead of combining the tomato sauce, chili powder, and cumin, pick up a can of red enchilada sauce in the Latino section of your grocery store. Also, you might experiment with using a cup of mixed shredded cheeses – a "Mexican" combination of shredded cheeses are available in the refrigerated cheese section of your market. This combination will give added flavor to this dish.

# Your Shopping List:

- ☐ 1 8-oz.can of tomato sauce
- ☐ 8 eggs
- ☐ 1 8-oz. package of shredded cheddar cheese
- ☐ 1 package of prepared tostada shells

## From Your Pantry:

- ☐ chili powder, cumin, black pepper, cayenne pepper, cooking spray, aluminum foil

# Maple Syrup Baked Pears

| | |
|---|---|
| 2 T. | butter |
| 4 large | pears |
| 1/2 c. | pure maple syrup |
| 1/2 t. | ground cinnamon |
| 1/2 c. | walnuts, chopped |

Preheat the oven to 350°F. Butter an 8" x 11" baking dish. Cut the pears in half, and remove the core and the peel. Place the pears cut-side down in the buttered baking dish. Pour the maple syrup over the pears and sprinkle them with the cinnamon. Bake uncovered for 25 minutes or until the pears are tender when pierced with a fork. Sprinkle each pear with the walnut pieces. Serve warm. Makes 8 servings.

Kids can help with this recipe:

1. Butter the baking dish.
2. Wash the pears.
3. Older kids can peel the pears with a child-safe peeler.
4. Measure the maple syrup and pour over the pears in the baking dish.
5. Measure and sprinkle cinnamon over the pears.
6. Measure and sprinkle the walnut pieces over the baked pears.

## quick tip

Rather than going to the store to pick up some pears, you can use up any extra apples or even bananas that you may have. You can also use chopped hazelnuts or sliced almonds as an alternative to the walnuts. This is a dish for which you may already have all the ingredients at home!

**Teachable Moment:** This is a great opportunity to teach your child helper that maple syrup comes from the sap of the maple tree. American Indians taught the Colonists how to tap the maple tree for its sap and boil the sap to form maple syrup. It takes between 20 and 50 gallons of maple sap to make 1 gallon of maple syrup.

# Your Shopping List:

- ☐ 4 large pears
- ☐ 1 package of walnuts

## From Your Pantry:

- ☐ butter, pure maple syrup, cinnamon

## Creamy Berry Smoothie

| | |
|---|---|
| 1 c. | frozen raspberries |
| 1/2 c. | frozen blackberries |
| 1/2 c. | frozen boysenberries |
| 1 c. | fat-free mixed berry yogurt |
| 1/2 c. | grape juice |

Pour the berries, yogurt, and the grape juice into a blender. Blend until smooth and creamy. Serve cold. Makes 2 servings.

### quick tip

Smoothies are quick, fuss-free, and kid-friendly. Feel free to experiment with any extra fruit such as strawberries, peaches, melon, and mango that you might already have on hand. Orange juice and fruit nectars are great additions. You can also use ripe bananas or fat-free sherbets for an even creamier texture. Yum!

Kids can help with this recipe:

1. Measure all of the ingredients and place in the blender.
2. With supervision, blend the ingredients until smooth.

# Your Shopping List:

- ☐ 1 container of frozen raspberries
- ☐ 1 container of frozen blackberries
- ☐ 1 container of frozen boysenberries (or 1 large container of mixed berries)
- ☐ 1 container of fat-free mixed berry yogurt
- ☐ 1 container of grape juice

## BBQ Smoked Chicken Pizza

| 1 12-inch | prepared pizza shell (or homemade pizza dough, if desired) |
| 1 c. | prepared barbecue sauce |
| 1/2 lb. | deli-style smoked chicken, in small chunks |
| 1 c. | red onion, thinly sliced into rings |
| 2 T. | fresh Italian flat-leaf parsley, finely minced |
| 3 c. | mozzarella cheese, shredded |

Place the pizza shell or prepared dough on a baking sheet that has been sprinkled with cornmeal. Heat the oven to 400°F. Spread the barbecue sauce on the pizza shell and layer the smoked chicken over the sauce. Scatter the onion rings over the chicken and sprinkle the parsley on top of the onion. Spread the mozzarella cheese over all. Bake the pizza for 12 to15 minutes, or until the cheese is melted and the pizza is bubbly. Makes 6 servings.

Kids can help with this recipe:

1. Spread the barbecue sauce on the pizza shell/dough.
2. Wash the flat-leaf parsley.
3. Layer the chicken, onion rings, and parsley.
4. Sprinkle the mozzarella cheese over the pizza.

## Your Shopping List:

❑ 1 12-inch prepared pizza shell (or ingredients for homemade pizza dough, if desired)
❑ 1 jar of prepared barbecue sauce
❑ 1/2 lb. deli-style pre-cooked smoked chicken
❑ 1 small red onion
❑ 1 bunch of fresh Italian flat-leaf parsley
❑ 1 large bag of shredded mozzarella cheese

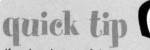

## quick tip

If you love the taste of pizza crust made from fresh dough but don't like to make the dough at home, stop by your neighborhood pizzeria and ask to buy just the dough from them. It's easy, inexpensive, and will help you create a restaurant-quality pizza with the perfect crust.

# Chicken Chilaquiles

| | |
|---|---|
| 3 c. | cooked chicken, cubed |
| 4 | green onions, finely sliced |
| 1 7-oz. | can chopped green chilies |
| 2 12-oz. | cans cream of chicken soup |
| 2 c. | dairy sour cream |
| 6 oz. | seasoned tortilla chips |
| 4 oz. | cheddar cheese, shredded |

Lightly coat a 2-quart baking pan with cooking spray. In a large bowl, combine the chicken, onions, chilies, and cream of chicken soup. Mix thoroughly. Add the sour cream and mix again. Place the tortilla chips in the bottom of the baking pan and pour the chicken over the chips. Sprinkle the cheddar cheese over the chicken. Bake, uncovered, at 350°F for 30 minutes. Makes 6 servings.

Kids can help with this recipe:

1. If using rotisserie chicken, kids can remove and measure the meat from the bones.
2. Coat the baking pan with cooking spray.
3. Wash the green onions.
4. With supervision, older children can open the cans of green chilies and soup with a can opener and place contents in a large mixing bowl.
5. Combine the chicken, green onions, chilies, soup, and sour cream in the mixing bowl.
6. Place the tortilla chips on the bottom of the baking pan.
7. Help pour the chicken mixture over the tortilla chips.
8. Measure and sprinkle the cheese over the chicken.

**quick tip**

This is a great recipe to use with leftover chicken or even turkey from a previous meal. However, if you don't have leftovers, swing by your supermarket deli and pick up a pre-cooked rotisserie chicken. Remove the meat and use it to create this delicious dish.

**Teachable Moment:** Kids will be interested to learn that chilaquiles is a Mexican dish that was invented to use leftovers.

# Your Shopping List:

- ❑ 1 pre-cooked rotisserie chicken
- ❑ 1 bunch of green onions, finely sliced
- ❑ 1 7-oz. can of green chilies, chopped
- ❑ 2 12-oz. cans of cream of chicken soup
- ❑ 1 container of dairy sour cream
- ❑ 1 large bag of tortilla chips
- ❑ 1 8-oz. bag of shredded cheddar cheese

## From Your Pantry:

- ❑ cooking spray

# Turkey & Walnut Couscous with Cranberry Sauce

| | |
|---|---|
| 1 6-oz. | pkg. couscous pasta, with herb seasoning packet |
| 1-1/4 c. | chicken stock |
| 1 T. | butter or margarine |
| 1-1/2 c. | cooked turkey, cubed |
| 1/4 c. | walnuts, chopped |
| 1/2 t. | freshly ground black pepper |
| 1 t. | fresh sage, chopped |

**Cranberry Sauce:**

| | |
|---|---|
| 1 c. | canned cranberry sauce |
| 2 T. | fresh apple juice |

Combine the couscous, chicken stock, and butter in a large saucepan. Bring to a boil. Add the seasoning packet, turkey, walnuts, and pepper and stir to combine. Remove the saucepan from the heat and allow it to stand for 7 minutes. In a 2-cup glass measuring cup, heat the cranberry sauce and apple juice in the microwave oven for 1 minute on high. Spoon the sauce over the cooked turkey couscous. Sprinkle with fresh sage. Makes 4 servings.

## quick tip

Despite looking like a grain, couscous is actually a type of pasta that hails from North Africa. It is extremely versatile and cooks in less than 10 minutes. Couscous comes in many forms and sizes from plain to a variety of seasoned packets. Try using couscous as a quick alternative to rice in non-Asian dishes.

Kids can help with this recipe:

1. Measure the butter and chicken stock and add to the saucepan.
2. Open the couscous package, remove the seasoning packet, and add the couscous to the saucepan.
3. Measure the turkey, walnut pieces, and black pepper and add to the hot couscous.
4. Measure the cranberry sauce and apple juice.
5. Sprinkle the fresh sage.

# Your Shopping List:

- ❑ 1 14-oz. can of chicken stock
- ❑ 1 6-oz. package of couscous pasta with herb seasoning packet
- ❑ 3/4 lb. cooked turkey
- ❑ 1 small package of walnuts
- ❑ 1 sprig of fresh sage
- ❑ 1 can of whole-berry cranberry sauce
- ❑ 1 small container of apple juice

## From Your Pantry:
- ❑ butter or margarine, black pepper

# Beef Tamale Pie

| | |
|---|---|
| 1 small | yellow onion, chopped |
| 1/2 lb. | ground beef |
| 1 c. | canned chili beans |
| 1 8-oz. | can tomato sauce |
| 1 c. | frozen corn kernels, defrosted |
| 2 T. | ground chili powder |
| 1/2 t. | salt |
| 1 8-oz. | pkg. cornbread mix |
| 1 c. | milk |
| 1 | egg, beaten |

In a large skillet on medium heat, sauté the onion and ground beef together until beef is browned and onion is translucent. Season with salt and pepper to taste.

In a large baking pan, stir together the chili beans, tomato sauce, corn, chili powder, salt, and ground beef mixture. Preheat the oven to 350°F. In a small bowl, mix the cornbread mix, milk, and egg and spread the batter evenly over the chili. Bake, uncovered, for 30 minutes or until the cornbread is completely cooked and the chili is heated through. Makes 4 servings.

Kids can help with this recipe:

1. Older kids, with supervision, can open the cans of chili beans and tomato sauce with a can opener.
2. Measure the chili beans, corn, ground chili powder, salt, and combine with the tomato sauce and ground beef mixture in a large baking pan.
3. Beat the egg.
4. Mix together the cornbread mix, milk, and beaten egg.

**Teachable Moment:** Chili is the official dish of Texas. It can be smoky, spicy, sweet, and savory. Some prefer chili with just beans; others like it with the addition of ground meat. Americans eat an average of 15 pounds of beans a year.

# Your Shopping List:

- ❑ 1 small yellow onion
- ❑ 1/2 lb. ground beef
- ❑ 1 can of your favorite chili beans
- ❑ 1 8-oz. can of tomato sauce
- ❑ 1 small package of frozen corn kernels
- ❑ 1 8-oz. package of cornbread mix
- ❑ 1 egg

## From Your Pantry:

- ❑ ground chili powder, salt, milk

## quick tip

If you have leftover chicken or turkey, you can use this instead of the ground beef. You could also add a diced jalapeño pepper for added oomph.

# Linguine Asiago

| | |
|---|---|
| 8-oz. | fresh linguine noodles |
| 2 T. | extra-virgin olive oil |
| 1 | red bell pepper, finely chopped |
| 2 cloves | garlic, minced |
| 1/2 c. | Asiago cheese, grated |
| 1/4 t. | dried red pepper flakes |
| 2 T. | fresh Italian flat-leaf parsley, minced |

Cook the noodles in boiling water until they are just tender. Drain and place the noodles in a large serving bowl. While noodles are still hot, add the olive oil, red pepper, garlic, cheese, and parsley. Toss well and serve immediately. Makes 3 to 4 servings.

Kids can help with this recipe:

1. Wash the red bell pepper and deseed.
2. Wash the parsley.
3. Mince the garlic in a garlic press.
4. Measure the olive oil, cheese, red pepper flakes, and parsley.

# Your Shopping List:

- ❑ 1 8-oz. package of fresh linguine noodles
- ❑ 1 medium red bell pepper, finely chopped
- ❑ 1 container of freshly grated Asiago cheese (or a 2 oz. block of Asiago)
- ❑ 1 bunch of fresh Italian flat-leaf parsley

## From Your Pantry:

- ❑ extra-virgin olive oil, garlic, red pepper flakes

## quick tip

Fresh pasta in the refrigerated section of grocery stores is a great timesaver. These pastas generally take only a few minutes to cook and have a soft, buttery quality to them. Try the fresh ravioli, tortellini, and spaghetti, to name a few.

# Pepperoni Pizza Bagels

| | |
|---|---|
| 1 6 oz. | can tomato paste |
| 1 t. | ground oregano |
| 5 | fresh plain or savory bagels, split |
| 1/2 c. | onion, chopped |
| 1/2 c. | green bell pepper, chopped |
| 1 c. | pepperoni slices, chopped |
| 1 c. | mozzarella cheese, shredded |

Preheat the oven to 450°F. Combine the tomato paste and oregano in a small bowl. Spread equal portions of the tomato sauce over each of the bagel halves and arrange the bagel halves on a baking sheet. Top each bagel with onions, green peppers and the chopped pepperoni. Sprinkle the cheese over each bagel. Bake for 6 to 8 minutes and serve immediately. Makes 5 servings.

Kids can help with this recipe:

1. Older kids can, with supervision, open the can of tomato paste with a can opener.
2. Measure the dried oregano and combine with the tomato paste.
3. Spread the tomato paste mixture over each bagel half.
4. Wash and deseed the green bell pepper.
5. Measure the shredded mozzarella cheese.
6. Top the bagel halves with onion, green pepper, pepperoni, and cheese.

**Teachable Moment:** Your child helper will be interested to know that bagels are a Jewish doughnut-shaped roll that is boiled in water before being baked. The word "bagel" comes from the German word "beugel," which means ring or bracelet.

## quick tip

This recipe is a great way to use up any left-over plain or savory bagels. (Just make sure you don't use any sweet-flavored bagels, such as blueberry or cinnamon raisin!) You could also use sourdough hoagie rolls. In addition, salami is a great substitute for the pepperoni.

# Your Shopping List:

- ❑ 1 6-oz. can of tomato paste
- ❑ 1 bag of plain or savory fresh bagels (at least 5 bagels)
- ❑ 1 small white onion
- ❑ 1 medium green bell pepper
- ❑ 1/2 lb. pepperoni slices
- ❑ 1 small package of shredded mozzarella cheese

## From Your Pantry:

- ❑ ground oregano

# Pasta e Fagioli

| | |
|---|---|
| 1 16-oz. | can crushed tomatoes, Italian-style |
| 1 19-oz. | can cannelloni beans, rinsed and drained |
| 1/2 c. | fresh green beans, trimmed and cut into 1-inch lengths |
| 1 small | white onion, chopped |
| 2 cloves | garlic, minced |
| 5 c. | vegetable broth |
| 1 small | zucchini, cut into thin slices |
| 1 c. | uncooked small shell macaroni |
| 1 t. | salt |
| 1 t. | black pepper |
| 1/2 t. | crushed red pepper |
| | fresh Parmesan cheese for garnish |

Combine in a large stockpot the tomatoes, beans, green beans, onion, garlic, and vegetable broth. Stir over medium heat for 6 minutes. Add the zucchini, macaroni, salt, black pepper, and red pepper and stir again. Simmer for 20 minutes to combine the flavors. Sprinkle Parmesan cheese over each serving. Makes 4 servings.

Kids can help with this recipe:

1. Older kids, with supervision, can open the cans of crushed tomatoes, cannelloni beans, and vegetable broth with a can opener, and then they can place the contents in a large stockpot.

2. Clean the green beans and snap off the ends.

3. Mince the garlic in a garlic press.

4. Clean the zucchini.

5. Measure the macaroni, salt, black pepper, and red pepper, and add them to the stockpot.

6. Sprinkle Parmesan cheese over each serving.

# Your Shopping List:

- 1 16-oz. can of crushed tomatoes, Italian-style
- 1 19-oz. can of cannelloni beans
- 1/2 c. fresh green beans
- 1 small white onion
- 2 cloves of garlic
- 3 cans of vegetable broth
- 1 small zucchini
- 1 package of small shell macaroni
- fresh Parmesan cheese (for garnish)

## From Your Pantry:

- garlic, salt, black pepper, crushed red pepper

## quick tip

This is the dish in which to use frozen vegetables for added convenience. Frozen green beans, pearl onions, and diced carrots are easy substitutes for the fresh vegetables.

# Caribbean Orange Roughy with Couscous

| 1-1/2 lbs. | orange roughy fillets |
|---|---|
| 1 t. | Caribbean jerk seasoning |
| 1 T. | butter |
| 1/4 c. | orange-pineapple juice |
| 1 6-oz. | pkg. Parmesan cheese couscous |
| 1 | ripe orange, unpeeled, cut into thin slices |

Sprinkle the orange roughy fillets with the jerk seasoning, rubbing it in to adhere well. In a large sauté pan on medium high, melt the butter until foamy. Add the fish fillets and sear each side for about 1 minute each. Add the orange-pineapple juice and half of the orange slices, and cook on medium-low for another 6 minutes or until the fish is cooked through. Meanwhile, prepare the couscous according to package directions. To serve, scoop the couscous onto plates and top with the fillets. Garnish with the remaining fresh orange slices. Makes 4 servings.

Kids can help with this recipe:

1. Measure and rub the jerk seasoning onto the fish fillets.
2. Measure the orange-pineapple juice and add to the sauté pan.
3. Garnish the finished dish with fresh orange slices.

**Teachable Moment:** Orange roughy is a fish found near New Zealand. It doesn't reproduce until it is 30 years old! Because of this, it is important orange roughy is fished in a sustainable manner or soon it will disappear.

# Your Shopping List:

- ❑ 1-1/2 lbs. orange roughy fillets
- ❑ 1 pint orange-pineapple juice
- ❑ 1 6-oz. package of couscous
- ❑ 1 ripe orange

## From Your Pantry:

- ❑ Caribbean jerk seasoning, butter

## quick tip

This is a great dish for any type of fish that you have in your freezer or is on sale at the market. Ahi tuna, salmon, and tilapia are some varieties that come to mind. Just make sure to cook the fish for the required amount of time, altering cooking time by thickness.

# Broccoli Beef with Fresh Mushrooms

| | |
|---|---|
| 1 T. | butter or margarine |
| 1 c. | fresh crimini or white mushrooms, sliced |
| 2 T. | white onion, finely chopped |
| 1 clove | garlic, minced |
| 1 lb. | cooked deli roast beef, cut into matchstick pieces |
| 1 t. | freshly ground black pepper |
| 1 10-3/4 oz. | can cream of mushroom soup |
| 2 c. | instant white rice |
| 1 c. | broccoli florets, cut into small pieces |

In a large skillet, heat butter or margarine on medium-high heat until foamy. Sauté the mushroom slices, onion, and garlic until mushrooms have softened and are slightly browned. Add the roast beef slices and pepper and heat through. Stir and add the cream of mushroom soup. Slowly stir in one soup can of water. Then add the rice and broccoli and cook over medium-high heat until the mixture boils. Cook without stirring over medium heat for 5 minutes. Remove from the heat, cover, and let sit for 5 minutes, or until the rice is cooked and the broccoli is tender-crisp. Makes 4 servings.

Kids can help with this recipe:

1. Measure the butter or margarine and place in the skillet.
2. Mince the garlic in a garlic press.
3. Measure the ground black pepper and add to the skillet.
4. Older kids can, with supervision, open the can of soup with a can opener.
5. Measure a soup can of water.
6. Measure the rice and broccoli and add to the hot skillet.

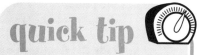

## quick tip

Your supermarket deli is a fantastic helper when you are planning a quick meal. Rather than asking for lunchmeat slices, you can always request that they cut off a whole portion of lunchmeat so you can cut it appropriately later. For this recipe, ask for 1 lb. of roast beef so that you can cut it into the matchstick pieces the dish requires.

# Your Shopping List:

- ❑ 1 c. fresh crimini or white mushrooms
- ❑ 1 small white onion
- ❑ 1 lb. cooked deli roast beef
- ❑ 1 10-3/4 oz. can of cream of mushroom soup
- ❑ 1 package of instant white rice
- ❑ 1 bag of broccoli florets

## From Your Pantry:

- ❑ butter, garlic, black pepper

# Crab & Cheese Muffin Melts

| | |
|---|---|
| 4 | English muffins, split |
| 1/2 c. | prepared tartar sauce |
| 3/4 lb. | fresh crab (you may substitute imitation crab, if desired) |
| 8 | slices ripe tomato |
| 8 | slices Monterey Jack cheese |
| | salt and pepper to taste |

Place the muffins on a large cookie or baking sheet. Preheat the oven broiler. Spread each muffin-half with tartar sauce and top with the crab. Sprinkle with salt and pepper to taste. Top each muffin with a slice of tomato and a slice of cheese. Broil the muffins for 3 to 4 minutes or until the cheese is bubbly and the crab is warmed through. Makes 4 servings.

Kids can help with this recipe:

1. Split the English muffins and place on a baking sheet.
2. Spread each muffin-half with tartar sauce.
3. Layer the crab, salt and pepper, tomato, and cheese slice on each muffin-half.

## quick tip

If fresh crab is unavailable or simply too expensive, you can also use canned lump crabmeat. Also, you can add a dash of hot pepper sauce to the tartar sauce for a livelier flavor.

# Your Shopping List:

- ☐ 1 package of English muffins
- ☐ 3/4 lb. fresh crab (you may substitute imitation crab, if desired)
- ☐ 1 large ripe tomato
- ☐ 8 slices of Monterey Jack cheese (from your supermarket deli)

## From Your Pantry:

- ☐ prepared tartar sauce, salt, black pepper

# Chicken & Zucchini Ziti

| | |
|---|---|
| 1 lb. | boneless, skinless chicken breasts |
| 2 T. | extra-virgin olive oil |
| 3 c. | ziti pasta, uncooked |
| 2 | zucchini, sliced thinly |
| 1 32-oz. | jar prepared spaghetti sauce with mushrooms and onion |
| 1 c. | water |
| 1 c. | mozzarella cheese |

Cut the chicken breasts into small cubes. Using a large, deep sauté pan with a dome lid, cook the chicken in the olive oil on medium heat until no pink remains. Add the ziti, zucchini, spaghetti sauce, and water and mix well. Sprinkle with the mozzarella cheese and reduce the heat to simmer. Cover and cook for 20 to 25 minutes or until the pasta is tender and the entrée is cooked through. Makes 4 servings.

Kids can help with this recipe:

1. Measure the olive oil and add to the sauté pan.
2. Measure the pasta and water and add to the sauté pan.
3. Add the sliced zucchini and the spaghetti sauce to the pan.
4. Sprinkle the dish with mozzarella cheese.

**Teachable Moment:** We always think of tomato-based pasta sauces as essential to Italian cooking, but did you know that tomatoes are native to North and South America? Italians didn't have access to tomatoes until Spaniards brought them to Europe after finding them in Mexico in 1519. At first, the Europeans thought they were poisonous but soon found a use for them in cooking. Now tomatoes are the third-most widely consumed vegetable in the United States.

# Your Shopping List:

- ❏ 1 lb. boneless, skinless chicken breasts
- ❏ 1 package of ziti pasta
- ❏ 2 large zucchini
- ❏ 1 32-oz. jar of prepared spaghetti sauce with mushrooms and onion
- ❏ 1 small package of shredded mozzarella cheese

## From Your Pantry:

- ❏ extra-virgin olive oil

## quick tip

By cooking the ziti pasta in the rest of the ingredients, not only do you save an extra step, but your pasta will take on the rich flavor of the spaghetti sauce. If you have leftover homemade marinara sauce, by all means use it in this delightful dish.

# Grilled Swordfish with Tomato-Dill Relish

**Tomato-Dill Relish:**

| | |
|---|---|
| 1 medium | ripe tomato, chopped |
| 1 | green onion, sliced |
| 1/4 c. | extra-virgin olive oil |
| 1/4 c. | Parmesan cheese, crumbled |
| 1 T. | fresh lemon juice |
| 1 T. | fresh dill, chopped |
| 1/4 t. | ground black pepper |

**Swordfish:**

| | |
|---|---|
| 1/4 c. | extra-virgin olive oil |
| 1/4 c. | Dijon mustard |
| 2 T. | red wine |
| 1 clove | garlic, minced |
| 1 t. | ground basil |
| 1/2 t. | salt |
| 4 | swordfish steaks, 6 to 8 ounces each |

In a medium bowl, combine the tomato, green onion, olive oil, Parmesan cheese, lemon juice, dill weed, and black pepper. Mix well and set aside.

In a small bowl, combine the olive oil, Dijon mustard, red wine, garlic, basil and the salt, stirring well. Brush both sides of the swordfish steaks with the sauce. Grill the fish over medium-high heat, 6 to 8 minutes on each side, until cooked through. Baste frequently with the mustard sauce. Place a large spoonful of Tomato-Dill Relish on four individual plates. Top the relish with the grilled swordfish and serve. Makes 4 servings.

Kids can help with this recipe:

1. Wash the tomato, green onion, and dill.
2. Squeeze the lemon for its juice and remove any seeds.
3. Measure the olive oil, Parmesan cheese, lemon juice, dill, and black pepper for the relish. Combine these ingredients with the tomato and green onion and mix well.

## quick tip

Completion of this dish becomes even faster when you prepare the component parts in advance. The night before, make the Tomato-Dill Relish and the swordfish mustard sauce and store separately in the refrigerator in resealable containers. The next day, the cooking of the fish will take less than 10 minutes!

4. Mince the garlic in a garlic press.

5. Measure the olive oil, Dijon mustard, red wine, basil, and salt for the mustard sauce. Add the garlic and mix well to combine.

6. Spoon the Tomato-Dill Relish onto each plate.

**Teachable Moment:** Let your child helper touch the dill and explain that it is an herb related to parsley. It can grow up to 3 feet tall and its delicate, feathery leaves and hard seeds are used as flavorings in cooking. Dill pickles get their name because dill is used in the pickle brine.

# Your Shopping List:

- ❑ 1 medium ripe tomato
- ❑ 1 bunch of green onions
- ❑ 1 container of freshly shredded Parmesan cheese
- ❑ 1 lemon
- ❑ 1 bunch of fresh dill
- ❑ 4 swordfish steaks, 6 to 8 ounces each

## From Your Pantry:

- ❑ Extra-virgin olive oil, ground black pepper, Dijon mustard, red wine, garlic, ground basil, salt

# It Only Takes A Few Ingredients

**3**

One timesaving strategy when cooking entrées is to use recipes that employ only a few, simple ingredients. All of the recipes in this chapter use less than eight basic ingredients to simplify the cooking process. Rather than forcing you to manage a multitude of ingredients and components, these recipes are so refreshingly straightforward that you can literally throw a few items together, and the resulting dishes are still mouth-wateringly good. Also, because only a few ingredients are used, these recipes are budget-friendly and give you good bang for your buck.

This chapter demonstrates the importance of flavor combinations. Honey and soy sauce, prosciutto and asparagus, parmesan cheese and spinach, green chile and lime…these basic flavor pairs (to name a few) are the keys to efficient cooking while maintaining spectacular taste. Once you've built a library of basic flavor combinations, you can create and alter your own recipes with ease.

By the end of this chapter, you will:

- create dishes that are simple but flavorful
- use only a few ingredients to produce each dish
- learn which flavor combinations are the best for quick cooking
- learn how to use the grill and microwave to expedite the cooking process
- employ your child helpers in the kitchen and teach them cooking skills
- wow your kids with exciting food facts

- make your grocery shopping even more efficient with our practical lists
- use your pantry as a great resource for limited-ingredient dishes
- rest assured that you have mastered a collection of easy, budget- and time-friendly dishes

# Honey & Garlic Spareribs

| | |
|---|---|
| 3 lbs. | pork spareribs |
| 1/4 t. | garlic salt |
| 1/2 c. | honey |
| 3 T. | cider vinegar |
| 1/4 t. | black pepper |
| 1/4 c. | soy sauce |
| 3 cloves | garlic, minced |

Preheat the oven to 350°F. Season the spareribs with the garlic salt. Cut the spareribs into individual ribs and arrange in a 13" x 9" baking dish. Cover with foil and bake in the oven for an hour. Drain off the liquid. In a saucepan, combine the honey, cider vinegar, black pepper, soy sauce, and the garlic and simmer for 5 minutes. Pour this honey mixture over the ribs and bake uncovered for 30 minutes. Baste every 10 minutes. Makes 20 appetizer servings.

Kids can help with this recipe:

1. Measure the garlic salt and sprinkle it over the spareribs.
2. Arrange the cut spareribs in the baking dish.
3. Mince the garlic in a garlic press.
4. Measure the honey, cider vinegar, black pepper, and soy sauce. Combine all ingredients with the garlic in a saucepan.

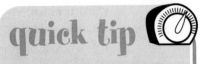

## quick tip

To speed the cooking process, you can parboil the ribs in water and/or beer for 30 minutes, skipping the foil-covered baking step. After draining, bake for 30 minutes with the honey mixture.

# Your Shopping List:

❑ 3 lbs. pork spareribs

## From Your Pantry:

❑ garlic salt, honey, cider vinegar, black pepper, soy sauce, garlic, aluminum foil

# Savory Pork Roast

| | |
|---|---|
| 2 lbs. | pork loin roast, boneless |
| 2 cloves | garlic, minced |
| 1/2 | yellow onion, chopped |
| 1/2 c. | soy sauce |
| 1/4 c. | chicken broth |
| 1/4 t. | black pepper |

Stab the pork roast on all sides with a fork. Mix together the garlic, onion, and soy sauce. Place the pork in a refrigerator container, pour the soy mixture over the meat, and then cover the meat with the black pepper. Refrigerate overnight. Preheat the oven to 350°F. Place the pork roast on a rack in a roasting pan and bake for approximately 1 hour or until the meat thermometer shows 135°F. Remove the meat from the oven. Let it sit for 15 minutes and then slice and serve. Makes 4 servings.

Kids can help with this recipe:

1. Stab the roast with a fork.
2. Mince the garlic with a garlic press.
3. Measure the chopped onion and soy sauce. Combine with the garlic. Pour over the roast.
4. Season the pork with black pepper.

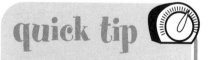

## quick tip

For a quicker version of this recipe, substitute pork tenderloin or pork chops. These can be grilled for a faster finish.

# Your Shopping List:

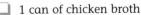

- ☐ 2 lbs. pork loin roast, boneless
- ☐ 1 small yellow onion
- ☐ 1 can of chicken broth

## From Your Pantry:

- ☐ garlic, soy sauce, black pepper

# Salmon with Hot Sweet Mustard

| 1 T. | extra-virgin olive oil |
|---|---|
| 5 to 6 lbs. | side of salmon |
| 1/2 c. | mayonnaise |
| 3 T. | hot sweet mustard |
| 1 t. | garlic, minced |
| | salt and pepper to taste |

Preheat the oven to 350°F. Lightly oil a large, shallow baking sheet. Wipe the salmon with damp paper towels. Place the fish on the baking sheet. Combine the mayonnaise, mustard, garlic, and salt and pepper and spread it evenly on both sides of the salmon. Bake for 20 minutes and then check for completion. Serve immediately. Makes 6 to 8 servings.

Kids can help with this recipe:

1. Wipe the salmon with damp paper towels.
2. Mince the garlic in a garlic press.
3. Measure and combine the mayonnaise, mustard, garlic, salt, and pepper.
4. Spread the mayonnaise mixture on the fish.

## quick tip

A quick way to check if your fish is ready is the knife test. Take a small knife and stick in the thickest part of the fish for several seconds. Carefully remove and place the knife blade on your upper lip. If the blade feels hot, then the fish is fully cooked. Another way to check is using an instant read thermometer. For moist fish, you will want an internal temperature of 125°F; drier fish has a temperature of 135°F.

**Teachable Moment:** Prepared mustard can be found in many forms and cultures. The color and heat of mustard depends on the type of mustard seed used. The hottest mustard is Chinese mustard; one of the mildest is American yellow mustard.

# Your Shopping List:

☐ 5 to 6 lbs. side of salmon

## From Your Pantry:

☐ extra-virgin olive oil, mayonnaise, hot sweet mustard, garlic, salt, pepper, paper towels

# Prosciutto-Wrapped Asparagus with Balsamic Vinaigrette

| | |
|---|---|
| 1 lb. | fresh asparagus spears, cleaned |
| 16 pieces | prosciutto, thinly sliced |
| 3 T. | prepared balsamic vinaigrette |
| | freshly ground black pepper |
| 12 | cherry tomatoes, halved or quartered |

Bring a large stockpot of water to a boil. Lower the asparagus into the water and cook for 1 minute until tender-crisp. Cook 2 minutes if the spears are thick. Immediately dip the asparagus in cold water to stop the cooking process and drain. Place one asparagus spear on top of a slice of prosciutto. Roll the prosciutto around the asparagus spear. Continue rolling until all asparagus spears have been wrapped in prosciutto. To serve, arrange the asparagus wraps on a platter and drizzle with the balsamic vinaigrette. Sprinkle with the freshly ground black pepper. Garnish with the cherry tomatoes. Makes 8 servings.

Kids can help with this recipe:

1. Clean the asparagus spears and snap off the tough ends.
2. Wrap the prosciutto around each asparagus spear.
3. Measure the balsamic vinaigrette and drizzle over the finished dish.
4. Measure and sprinkle the black pepper.
5. Garnish with the cherry tomatoes.

**Teachable Moment:** Asparagus is a unique vegetable that can be either green or white. When growing, each asparagus spear pokes up out of the ground and is harvested when tall enough. Asparagus spears that are covered when growing remain white whereas green asparagus spears are uncovered and have exposure to sunlight.

## Your Shopping List:

- ❑ 1 lb. fresh asparagus spears
- ❑ 16 pieces of prosciutto, thinly sliced
- ❑ 1 container of prepared balsamic vinaigrette
- ❑ 12 cherry tomatoes

### From Your Pantry:

- ❑ black pepper

## quick tip

Fire up the grill! Just rub the asparagus spears with extra-virgin olive oil, salt, and pepper. Throw the spears on a very hot grill – about 1 minute per side will suffice. Remove the asparagus before they get too soft. Grilling asparagus is quick, simple, and imparts a delicious, smoky quality. Let the spears cool before wrapping with prosciutto.

# Beef Tenderloin Steaks with Tarragon Cream Sauce

| | |
|---|---|
| 4 | beef tenderloin steaks, 4 to 6 ounces each |
| | salt and cracked pepper to taste |
| 2 T. | extra-virgin olive oil |
| 2 T. | butter |
| 1 small | white onion, chopped |
| 1/2 c. | button mushrooms, sliced |
| 2 t. | fresh tarragon, chopped (or 1/2 t. dried tarragon) |
| 1/2 c. | heavy cream |
| | tarragon leaves for garnish |

## quick tip

Make sure to buy the pre-sliced button mushrooms to save you an extra step. You can also use this tarragon cream sauce on other cuts of beef.

Sprinkle the steaks with salt and pepper. In a large skillet over medium heat, add the olive oil and butter. When the butter melts, turn up the heat and add the steaks. Sear the steaks for 5 minutes on each side; remove the steaks to a serving platter and keep warm.

Drain all the drippings except 2 tablespoons from the skillet. Sauté the onions and mushrooms in the skillet until tender. Add the tarragon. Gradually stir in the heavy cream, and cook until heated through. Do not allow the sauce to boil. Pour the sauce over the steaks to serve. Garnish with tarragon leaves. Makes 4 servings.

Kids can help with this recipe:

1. Sprinkle the steaks with salt and pepper.
2. Measure the olive oil and butter and add to the skillet.
3. Clean the mushrooms with a damp towel.
4. Measure the mushroom slices.
5. Clean and remove the tarragon leaves from the stems.
6. Measure the heavy cream.

# Your Shopping List:

- ☐ 4 beef tenderloin steaks, 4 to 6 ounces each
- ☐ 1 small white onion
- ☐ 1/2 c. button mushrooms
- ☐ 1 bunch of fresh tarragon (or dried tarragon)
- ☐ 1 pint heavy cream

## From Your Pantry:

- ☐ salt, black pepper, extra-virgin olive oil, butter, dried tarragon

# Texas-Style BBQ Roast & Red Rice

| | |
|---|---|
| 3 lbs. | beef chuck roast |
| 1/2 t. | salt |
| 1/2 t. | freshly ground black pepper |
| 1/2 c. | brown sugar |
| 2 c. | prepared barbecue sauce |
| 1/2 c. | ketchup |
| 1/4 c. | chili sauce |
| 8 c. | hot, cooked long grain white rice |

Place the roast in a large baking pan and season with salt and pepper. Cover with aluminum foil. Bake at 350°F for 1 hour. Drain the juices and discard. Cover the roast with a thin layer of brown sugar. In a small bowl, combine the barbecue sauce, ketchup, and chili sauce and pour over the roast. Bake, uncovered, at 325°F for 2 hours, basting occasionally with the sauce. To serve, pour the sauce over the hot rice and top with the roast beef. Makes 6 to 8 servings.

Kids can help with this recipe:

1. Measure the salt and pepper and sprinkle over the roast.
2. Measure the brown sugar.
3. Measure and combine prepared barbecue sauce, ketchup, and chili sauce.

# Your Shopping List:

- ☐ 3 lbs. beef chuck roast
- ☐ 1 18-oz. jar of prepared barbecue sauce
- ☐ 1 12-oz. jar of chili sauce
- ☐ 1 5-lb. package of long grain rice

## From Your Pantry:
- ☐ salt, black pepper, brown sugar, ketchup, aluminum foil

# quick tip

Instead of using brown sugar, ketchup, and chili sauce, you can use a prepared spicy honey barbecue sauce to baste the roast.

# Kielbasa & Potato Skillet

| | |
|---|---|
| 2 T. | vegetable oil |
| 4 large | potatoes, peeled and cubed |
| 1 lb. | cooked Polish kielbasa, cut into 1/2-inch thick slices |
| 1 | onion, sliced |
| 1 t. | salt |
| 1/2 t. | freshly ground black pepper |
| 1 c. | frozen green peas, thawed and drained |

Heat the oil in a large sauté pan and add the potatoes. Season with salt to taste. Cook over medium-high heat for 5 minutes or until browned. Turn once. Add the sausage and onion and continue cooking for 2 minutes. Sprinkle the sausage and onions with the salt and pepper and add the green peas. Cook for 2 to 3 minutes and serve immediately. Makes 4 servings.

Kids can help with this recipe:

1. Measure the vegetable oil and add to the skillet.
2. Older kids can, with supervision, peel the potatoes with a child-safe vegetable peeler.
3. Measure the salt, pepper, and green peas and add to the skillet.

# Your Shopping List:

- ☐ 4 large potatoes
- ☐ 1 lb. Polish kielbasa
- ☐ 1 medium onion
- ☐ 1 16-oz. package of frozen peas

## From Your Pantry:

- ☐ vegetable oil, salt, black pepper

## quick tip

Before cooking the potatoes in the sauté pan, place them in an ovenproof bowl, cover with plastic wrap, and pop them into the microwave. Cook them on high for 2 to 3 minutes to soften them. This will reduce the overall cooking time.

# Parmesan Turkey Tenderloin with Spinach

| 1 10-3/4 oz. | can condensed cream of mushroom soup |
| 1/4 c. | half and half cream |
| 1 10-oz. | pkg. frozen spinach, thawed and squeezed dry |
| 6 large | slices turkey tenderloin |
| 1/2 c. | Parmesan cheese, grated |
| | freshly ground black pepper to taste |

Lightly coat a 9" x 13" baking pan with cooking spray. Combine the cream of mushroom soup with the half and half cream, and pour half of the mixture into the bottom of the pan. Arrange the spinach evenly over the soup and cover the spinach with the turkey slices. Pour the remaining soup mixture over the turkey. Spread the cheese over the turkey. Cover and bake at 350°F for 20 to 25 minutes or until the turkey is cooked completely through. Makes 4 to 6 servings.

Kids can help with this recipe:

1. Apply cooking spray to the baking pan.
2. Older kids can, with supervision, open the can of soup with a can opener.
3. Measure the cream and combine with the soup. Pour half of the mixture in the baking pan.
4. Arrange the spinach and turkey slices. Pour the remaining soup mixture on top of the turkey.
5. Measure the cheese and sprinkle on top of the dish.

**Teachable Moment:** Spinach is considered a "super vegetable" because of all the important nutrients it packs in! It contains plenty of vitamin A, C, fiber, and phytochemical lutein. Lutein is especially important to protect and maintain eyesight. Eat lots of spinach for strong eyes.

# Your Shopping List:

- ☐ 1 10-3/4 oz. can of condensed cream of mushroom soup
- ☐ 1 pint of half and half cream
- ☐ 1 10-oz. package of frozen spinach
- ☐ 6 large slices of turkey tenderloin
- ☐ 1 5-oz. container of freshly grated Parmesan cheese

## quick tip

You can ask your butcher to cut the turkey tenderloin into slices to expedite your recipe.

# From Your Pantry:

- ☐ black pepper, cooking spray

# Onion Baked Chicken & New Potatoes

| | |
|---|---|
| 6 | new red potatoes, cut into chunks |
| 8 pieces | chicken, as desired |
| 1 10-3/4 oz. | can condensed cream of chicken soup |
| 1/2 c. | chicken broth |
| 1 1-1/2 oz. | pkg. dry onion soup mix |

Place the potatoes in the bottom of a 9" x 13" baking pan. Arrange the chicken pieces over the potatoes. In a small bowl, mix together the soup, broth, and dry onion soup mix. Pour the soup mixture over the chicken and potatoes. Cover tightly with aluminum foil and bake at 375°F for 45 to 55 minutes or until the chicken is cooked through completely and the potatoes are tender. Makes 4 servings.

Kids can help with this recipe:

1. Place the potatoes and chicken pieces in the baking pan.
2. Older kids can, with supervision, open the cans of soup and broth with a can opener.
3. Combine the soup, broth, and dry onion mix in a small bowl. Pour over the chicken and potatoes.

# Your Shopping List:

- ❑ 6 medium new red potatoes
- ❑ 8 pieces of chicken
- ❑ 1 10-3/4 oz. can of condensed cream of chicken soup
- ❑ 1 14-oz. can of chicken broth
- ❑ 1 2-oz. package of dry onion soup mix

## From Your Pantry:
- ❑ aluminum foil

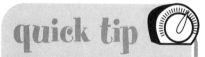

**quick tip**

If you cut the potatoes into small pieces and use boneless chicken breasts or boneless chicken thighs, you can reduce the cooking time of this satisfying dish by 10 minutes.

# Tortellini Florentine

| | |
|---|---|
| 1 28-oz. | jar prepared spaghetti sauce |
| 1 4-1/2 oz. | jar mushrooms, sliced |
| 1 lb. | fresh cheese tortellini (you may substitute frozen, thawed tortellini) |
| 1 10-oz. | pkg. frozen chopped spinach, thawed and squeezed dry |
| 1/2 c. | Parmesan cheese, grated |

Coat a 2-quart baking pan with cooking spray. Pour enough spaghetti sauce on the bottom of the pan to cover it. Add one half of the mushrooms. Layer one half of the cheese tortellini over the mushrooms and spread one half of the spinach over the tortellini. Pour one half of the remaining sauce over the spinach. Repeat the layers of mushrooms, tortellini, spinach, and sauce. Spread the Parmesan cheese over the sauce and bake, covered, at 350°F for 30 to 35 minutes or until heated through and bubbly. Makes 4 to 6 servings.

Kids can help with this recipe:

1. Apply cooking spray to the baking pan.
2. Open the jars of spaghetti sauce and mushrooms.
3. Layer the sliced mushrooms, cheese tortellini, spinach, and sauce as directed in the recipe.
4. Spread the Parmesan cheese over the final layer.

# Your Shopping List:

- ❑ 1 28-oz. jar of prepared spaghetti sauce
- ❑ 1 4-1/2 oz. jar of mushrooms
- ❑ 1 lb. fresh cheese tortellini (you may substitute frozen, thawed tortellini)
- ❑ 1 10-oz. package of frozen chopped spinach
- ❑ 1 5-oz. container of freshly grated Parmesan cheese

## From Your Pantry:
- ❑ cooking spray

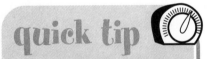

## quick tip

Fresh cheese tortellini only takes minutes to cook and is a delicious timesaver. You could also use flavored tortellini, flavored ravioli, or cheese ravioli in this scrumptious dish.

# Shrimp Personal Pizza Squares

| | |
|---|---|
| 1 10-oz. | pkg. refrigerated pizza dough |
| 4 medium | cherry tomatoes, cleaned and sliced |
| 6 oz. | cooked shrimp, peeled, deveined, and halved lengthwise |
| 1 T. | fresh oregano, chopped |
| 1/8 t. | crushed red pepper |
| 1 c. | mozzarella cheese, shredded |

Preheat the oven to 425°F. Roll the pizza dough into a 13-1/2" x 9" rectangle on a lightly floured surface. Cut the dough into six 4-1/2-inch squares. Place the squares 1 inch apart on a lightly greased cookie sheet. Bake for 4 to 5 minutes. Remove from the oven and keep the squares on the cookie sheet. On each pizza square, place 3 to 4 tomato slices. Top each square with 4 to 6 pieces of shrimp. Sprinkle the top of the shrimp with oregano and red pepper. Top with the shredded mozzarella cheese. Put the pizza squares back into the oven and bake a few minutes more until the cheese melts. To serve, place the pizza squares on a serving platter. Makes 6 servings.

Kids can help with this recipe:

1. Place the pizza dough squares on the cookie sheet.
2. Wash the tomatoes and oregano.
3. Layer each pizza square with tomato slices and shrimp.
4. Measure oregano and crushed red pepper and sprinkle on the squares.
5. Measure the mozzarella cheese and place on the pizza squares.

# Your Shopping List:

- ❑ 1 10-oz. package of refrigerated pizza dough
- ❑ 1 basket of large cherry tomatoes or 4 Roma tomatoes
- ❑ 1/2 lb. small shrimp, peeled and deveined
- ❑ 1 bunch of fresh oregano
- ❑ 1 8-oz. package of shredded mozzarella cheese

## From Your Pantry:

- ❑ crushed red pepper

## quick tip

Your market's seafood department carries pre-peeled, deveined shrimp. What a quick cook's helper! Rather than peeling and cleaning the fresh shrimp yourself, just buy the needed amount for the recipe. Or you can buy a bag of cleaned, frozen shrimp, utilize what you need, and keep the remaining shrimp in the bag, ready to be used with the next seafood recipe.

# Green Chile Chicken Breasts

| | |
|---|---|
| 1 c. | vegetable oil |
| 1/2 c. | lime juice |
| 3 T. | green chilies, seeded and chopped |
| 2 cloves | garlic, minced |
| 1/4 t. | salt |
| 6 | boneless, skinless chicken breast halves |
| | prepared salsa |

Combine the oil, juice, green chilies, garlic, and salt in a large, resealable plastic bag. Add the chicken halves and seal the bag. Refrigerate for 1 to 12 hours. Broil the chicken breasts for 6 minutes. Turn and broil for 6 more minutes or until cooked through completely. Serve with salsa. Makes 6 servings.

Kids can help with this recipe:

1. Measure the vegetable oil.

2. Squeeze the limes for juice.

3. Mince the garlic in a garlic press.

4. Measure the salt.

5. Combine the oil, lime juice, green chilies, garlic, and salt in a large, resealable plastic bag.

**Teachable Moment:** After salt, chile is the most frequently used seasoning in the world. The heat of the chile is caused by capsaicin, which is found in the seeds and seed membranes of the chile pepper. When removing the seed and membranes of chiles, be very careful and make sure to wash your hands with soap and water afterwards. Some chile peppers are mild and others are dangerously hot. If you ever eat a chile pepper that is too hot, drink a glass of milk; the milk will help to counteract the capsaicin oil and cool down your mouth.

# Your Shopping List:

- ☐ 6 ripe limes*
- ☐ 2 jalapeño chilies*
- ☐ 6 boneless, skinless chicken breast halves
- ☐ 1 16-oz. jar of prepared salsa

## From Your Pantry:

- ☐ vegetable oil, garlic, large resealable plastic bag

(*Or 1 16-oz. jar of chile verde)

## quick tip

Instead of using the oil, lime juice, green chilies, garlic, and salt, you can substitute the contents of a large jar of chile verde, which you can find in the Latino section of your grocery store. Though the flavorings are slightly different, it will still provide you with a spicy tanginess your family will enjoy.

# Cinnamon Apple Glazed Ham

| | |
|---|---|
| 1/4 c. | butter |
| 1/4 c. | brown sugar |
| 2 T. | Dijon mustard |
| 1 c. | canned apple pie filling |
| 1-1/2 lbs. | ham steaks, cut into 6 serving-sized portions |

Melt the butter in a large skillet and add the sugar and mustard. Cook over low heat for 1 minute. Add the apple pie filling, and cook and stir over medium heat for 5 minutes. Place the ham steaks in the skillet and cover with the apple mixture. Cook over medium heat for 5 minutes or until the ham is heated through. Serve the ham with the sauce on top. Makes 6 servings.

Kids can help with this recipe:

1. Measure the butter and place in the skillet.
2. Measure the brown sugar and mustard and place in the skillet with the melted butter.
3. Older kids can, with supervision, open the can of apple pie filling with a can opener.
4. Place the ham steaks in the skillet.

## Your Shopping List:

- ☐ 1 21 oz. can of apple pie filling
- ☐ 1-1/2 lbs. ham steaks

## From Your Pantry:

- ☐ butter, brown sugar, Dijon mustard

**quick tip**

Your butcher can come to the rescue. He or she will be happy to slice the ham steaks for you—-just ask! In addition, if you have it on hand, you can substitute 1 cup of apple-sauce and 1/2 tsp. of cinnamon for the apple pie filling.

## Macaroni with Creamy Cheese Sauce

| | |
|---|---|
| 8 oz. | elbow macaroni, cooked and drained |
| 2 c. | sharp cheddar cheese, shredded |
| 1 10-3/4 oz. | can cream of mushroom soup |
| 3/4 c. | milk |
| 1 t. | salt |
| 1 t. | black pepper |
| 1/2 cup | freshly grated Parmesan cheese |

Preheat the oven to 350°F. Grease or coat a large ovenproof serving pan with cooking spray. Combine the macaroni, cheddar cheese, and soup in the serving pan. Add the milk slowly along with the salt and pepper. Top with Parmesan cheese. Cover and bake for 30 to 35 minutes or until heated through and bubbly. Makes 6 servings.

Kids can help with this recipe:

1. Apply cooking spray to the serving pan.
2. Fill a large stockpot with water to cook the macaroni.
3. Older kids can, with supervision, open the can of soup with a can opener.
4. Measure the shredded cheddar cheese, milk, salt, and pepper.
5. Combine the macaroni, cheddar cheese, and soup in the serving pan.
6. Season with the salt and pepper.

**quick tip**

You can also add chopped ham, turkey, chicken, or even small, frozen, pre-cooked meatballs to this dish for added flavor and protein.

**Teachable Moment:** Macaroni and cheese is one of the most popular American comfort foods. "Wow" your child helper with this fun fact: Some historians think that Thomas Jefferson invented macaroni and cheese as we know it today. When he was president, Jefferson served it in the White House in 1802!

# Your Shopping List:

- ☐ 1 lb. package of elbow macaroni
- ☐ 1 8-oz. bag of shredded sharp cheddar cheese
- ☐ 1 10-3/4 oz. can of cream of mushroom soup
- ☐ 1 5-oz. container of freshly grated Parmesan cheese

## From Your Pantry:

- ☐ milk, salt, black pepper, cooking spray

# Smoked Salmon & Cream Cheese Quesadillas

| | |
|---|---|
| 4 10-inch | flour tortillas |
| 6 oz. | cream cheese, softened |
| 1 c. | smoked salmon, shredded |
| 1 | green onion, sliced |

Preheat the oven broiler. Place the tortillas on a large baking sheet and cover each with cream cheese. On one half of each tortilla, scatter the smoked salmon over the cheese and sprinkle the green onion over the salmon. Fold the tortilla over to form a half-circle with the smoked salmon sandwiched between the two layers of cream cheese. Broil for 3 minutes or until the cream cheese starts to bubble. Do not overcook. Makes 4 servings.

Kids can help with this recipe:

1. Take the cream cheese out to soften to room temperature.
2. Measure the smoked salmon.

## quick tip

Quesadillas are a perfect quick food. In addition to this elegant recipe, you can also create quesadillas using any leftover meats and cheeses you may have. Fresh herbs also enhance the flavors of this Tex-Mex staple. In fact, for this recipe, try substituting herb-flavored cream cheese for the plain cream cheese.

3. Scatter the smoked salmon and green onions over the tortillas, as directed.

4. Fold each tortilla over to form a half-circle.

# Your Shopping List:

- ❑ 1 8-count package of 10-inch flour tortillas
- ❑ 1 6-oz. package of cream cheese
- ❑ 1 8-oz. package of smoked salmon
- ❑ 1 bunch of green onions

# Roasted Green Chile Sirloin Burgers

| | |
|---|---|
| 1/2 cup | red onion, finely chopped |
| 3 tablespoons | roasted green chilies, chopped |
| 1 t. | salt |
| 1 t. | freshly ground black pepper |
| 1/4 t. | hot pepper sauce |
| 1-1/2 lbs. | beef ground sirloin |

Combine all of the ingredients except the ground sirloin in a medium bowl and toss to mix well. Add the ground sirloin and gently toss for two minutes with the other ingredients. Do not over mix or the beef will become tough. Lightly pat the beef into four patties, each about 3/4- to 1-inch thick. Grill over medium coals for 4 minutes. Turn once and grill for 5 to 6 minutes or until grilled as desired. Serve on toasted sourdough bread with your choice of condiments and toppings. Makes 4 servings.

Kids can help with this recipe:

1. Measure the red onion, green chilies, salt, black pepper, and hot pepper sauce, and combine in a mixing bowl.

2. Help you prepare any hamburger condiments (i.e. leaf lettuce, tomato slices, etc.).

**Teachable Moment:** The hamburger is one of the truly "American" dishes. Although its name is derived from Hamburg, Germany, the hamburger as we know it (a ground beef patty between two buns) was invented in the United States in the late 1800's. Many people have claimed they invented the hamburger, but no one knows for sure.

## quick tip

Instead of the various additions, you can simply add 1/4 cup of your favorite roasted salsa to the beef ground sirloin before forming the hamburger patties.

## Your Shopping List:

- ❑ 1 small red onion
- ❑ 1 7-oz. can of chopped roasted green chilies
- ❑ 1-1/2 pounds beef ground sirloin
- ❑ 1 package of sourdough rolls
- ❑ any favorite hamburger toppings (such as tomato and lettuce)

## From Your Pantry:

- ❑ salt, black pepper, hot pepper sauce, condiments

# Sicilian Grilled Chicken & Garlic

| 3 to 4 lbs. | roasting chicken, backbone split and wing tips removed |
| 2 t. | ground oregano |
| 2 t. | salt |
| 2 t. | freshly ground black pepper |
| 6 cloves | garlic, finely minced |

Place the chicken in a large glass pan, pressing down to flatten it as much as possible. Mix together the oregano, salt, pepper, and garlic in a small dish. Spread the herbs and garlic over the chicken. Turn and press the chicken and spread the remaining rub over it. Cover tightly with plastic wrap and refrigerate for 1 hour or up to 4 hours.

Grill the chicken over medium-low coals for 30 to 40 minutes. Turn the chicken every 15 minutes and avoid burning the skin. When the chicken is completely cooked, remove to a cutting board and let stand for 5 minutes. Carve the chicken and serve. Makes 4 servings.

Kids can help with this recipe:

1. Mince the garlic in a garlic press.
2. Measure the oregano, salt, and pepper. Combine with the garlic.
3. Rub the garlic mixture all over the chicken.

**Teachable Moment:** Garlic is indigenous to Siberia! It had to survive the extreme Siberian temperatures and a short growing season, so its cloves are actually practical storehouses of food for the plant. After its discovery thousands of years ago, garlic was dispersed throughout the world and is used in many ethnic cuisines. California is the world's largest producer of garlic, growing over 500 million pounds of garlic a year.

# Your Shopping List:

❏ 3 to 4 lbs. roasting chicken

## From Your Pantry:

❏ ground oregano, salt, black pepper, garlic, plastic wrap

## quick tip

Instead of applying to a whole split chicken, you can also use this Sicilian garlic rub on chicken pieces or even boneless chicken breasts.

# Bacon & Egg Breakfast Pitas

| | |
|---|---|
| 3 slices | Canadian bacon, diced |
| 3 | eggs |
| 1 T. | chives, minced |
| 1 | whole-wheat pita bread |
| 1/4 c. | cheddar cheese, grated |

In a skillet over medium heat, brown the Canadian bacon. Place the cooked bacon on a paper towel to remove any excess fat. In a small bowl, lightly mix the eggs and chives. Return the skillet to the heat, and then scramble the eggs and the Canadian bacon together until set. Top the egg and bacon combination with cheddar cheese.

In a separate skillet, warm the pita bread on low. Remove the pita from the skillet and cut it in half. Fill each half with the egg and bacon scramble. Serve warm. Makes 2 servings.

Kids can help with this recipe:

1. Wash the chives.
2. Crack open the eggs and blend with the chives.
3. Measure the cheddar cheese.

**Teachable Moment:** Your child helper will enjoy hearing about pita bread and its connection to the Middle East. Nomadic tribes in large caravans of camels, goats, and sheep would travel from place to place and could only take food that was easily transportable. Pita bread could be made in the camps and carried with them. It is made of flour, water, and a little salt, and it can be cooked in a pan over a campfire.

# Your Shopping List:

- ❑ 1 6-oz. package of Canadian bacon
- ❑ 3 eggs
- ❑ 1 bunch of chives
- ❑ 1 12-oz. package of whole wheat pita bread
- ❑ 1 8-oz. package of shredded cheddar cheese

## quick tip

Pita bread is a great base for many speedy dishes. You can stuff it with eggs and bacon(as in this recipe) or with lunchmeats, cheese, and vegetables for a low-carb sandwich. By adding salami, cheese, and tomato sauce, you can also create a quick stuffed pizza!

# Barbecue Hot Strips

| | |
|---|---|
| 4 | boneless, skinless, chicken breasts, cut into strips |
| 1-1/2 c. | prepared barbecue sauce |
| 2 t. | dry onion flakes |
| | hot pepper sauce to taste |

Spray a large skillet with cooking spray. Brown the chicken strips for 2 to 3 minutes on each side over medium heat, turning once and stirring occasionally. Add the barbecue sauce, onion, and hot pepper sauce to the skillet. Stir and simmer until the liquid is reduced by half and the sauce has thickened. Serve warm. Makes 8 servings.

Kids can help with this recipe:

1. Apply cooking spray to a large skillet.
2. Measure the barbecue sauce and dry onion flakes and add to the skillet.

## Your Shopping List:

☐ 4 boneless, skinless, chicken breasts

## From Your Pantry:

☐ prepared barbecue sauce, dry onion flakes, hot pepper sauce, cooking spray

## quick tip

You can save yourself the added step of cutting the chicken breasts into strips by simply buying a package of chicken tenderloins. Chicken tenderloins are an easy cut of poultry ideally suited for quick cooking. Use them to make chicken strips or cut them into smaller pieces for stir-fries.

# It Only Takes
# A Touch of Home

**O**n a cold, rainy night or after a particularly stressful day, satisfying comfort food is what you and your family crave. However, that traditional slow-simmered meal or a leisurely prepared, multi-step entrée just doesn't jive with your frenetic pace of life. This chapter provides you with recipes that give you that down-home taste without the slow pace of preparation. You will appreciate that these dishes show you how to cut corners without losing time-honored flavor and texture. As you master these recipes, your family and friends will be amazed that you can create delectable comfort foods in a limited amount of time with little effort.

By the end of this chapter, you will:

- create traditional comfort foods in a short amount of time
- learn kitchen shortcuts that minimize time but capture the flavor of down-home favorites
- discover which recipe components can be prepared in advance
- know how canned and frozen vegetables can still impart full flavor
- use leftovers as components in many recipes
- entertain and educate your child helpers with food trivia and history
- teach certain food preparation tasks to your child helpers
- streamline your grocery shopping with our handy lists
- value your well-stocked pantry
- add traditional, comfort food recipes to your ready-to-go library of family favorites

# Fresh Chive & Dijon Deviled Eggs

| | |
|---|---|
| 24 | large hard-cooked eggs |
| 3/4 c. | sour cream |
| 1/4 c. | mayonnaise |
| 1/4 c. | fresh chives, chopped |
| 1/4 t. | red pepper sauce |
| 1 T. | Dijon mustard |
| 2 t. | fresh lemon juice |
| 1/2 t. | ground black pepper |
| 1/2 c. | ham, cooked and chopped |
| | chopped chives for garnish |

Peel the eggs and cut in half lengthwise. Scoop out the egg yolks into a large bowl. Chop 4 egg white halves and add them to the bowl of yolks. Set aside the remaining egg whites.

Into the bowl of egg yolks, add the sour cream, mayonnaise, chives, red pepper sauce, mustard, lemon juice, and black pepper. Mash with a fork until smooth. Fill the reserved egg white halves with the yolk mixture. Place the filled eggs on a platter. Top each egg with 1/4 teaspoon of chopped ham. Garnish with chopped chives. Cover and refrigerate prior to serving, and refrigerate any leftovers. Makes 20 servings.

Kids can help with this recipe:

1. Put water in a stockpot to boil the eggs.
2. Peel the eggs.
3. Squeeze the lemon for lemon juice. Remove any seeds.
4. Wash the chives.
5. Measure the sour cream, mayonnaise, chives, red pepper sauce, Dijon mustard, lemon juice, and black pepper. Add to the egg yolks.
6. With a fork, mash the above mixture until smooth.
7. Top each egg with chopped ham.
8. Garnish with a sprinkling of chopped chives.

## quick tip

Everyone has his or her own method of hard boiling eggs, but this one is the easiest. Bring a pot of water to boil. Carefully put in the eggs. (It's helpful to use a slotted spoon to lower the eggs into the water so they don't crack.) Cover and turn off the heat. After 18 minutes, remove the eggs from the hot water and place into an ice bath. And voilà...perfectly cooked hardboiled eggs!

# Your Shopping List:

- ❑ 2 dozen large eggs
- ❑ 1 8-oz. container of sour cream
- ❑ 1 bunch of fresh chives
- ❑ 1 ripe lemon
- ❑ 8 oz. cooked ham

## From Your Pantry:

- ❑ mayonnaise, hot pepper sauce, Dijon mustard, black pepper

# Hot & Spicy Southern Fried Wings

**Sauce:**

| | |
|---|---|
| 1/2 c. | Louisiana Hot Sauce® |
| 1/4 c. | margarine |
| 3/4 T. | white vinegar |
| 1 t. | onion powder |
| 1-1/2 t. | garlic, minced |
| 1/2 t. | Worcestershire sauce |
| 2 t. | hot pepper sauce |
| 1/4 t. | celery seed powder |
| 1/4 t. | red pepper flakes |
| 1/4 t. | cayenne pepper |
| 1/8 t. | garlic salt |
| 1/8 t. | black pepper |
| | oil for frying |
| 1 c. | all-purpose flour |
| 1 T. | paprika |
| 24 | chicken wings with tips removed (you may substitute chicken drummettes, if desired) |
| | blue cheese dressing |
| | celery stalks |

## quick tip

The spicy sauce for the wings can be made the night before and stored in an airtight container. In fact, they take on additional flavor as the spices marry together. Likewise, you can dredge the chicken wings in advance and keep refrigerated under plastic wrap.

In a saucepan over medium heat, add all of the sauce ingredients. Stir together well and heat until slightly bubbly (about 5 minutes). Set aside.

Heat the oil in a large heavy skillet over high heat until it reaches 375°F. Mix the flour and the paprika together in a medium bowl and dredge the wings thoroughly. Carefully place the chicken wings in a single layer in the skillet. Fry until crisp and golden brown (about 8 to 12 minutes), turning several times. Drain the wings on paper towels. Repeat with the remaining wings. While the fried wings are still hot, use tongs to dip them thoroughly in the sauce and then place them on a serving platter. Serve the wings warm with the blue cheese dressing and the celery stalks alongside. Makes 10 to 12 servings.

Kids can help with this recipe:

1. Measure all of the sauce ingredients and add them to the saucepan.
2. Measure and combine the flour and paprika.
3. With supervision, dredge the chicken wings in the flour mixture.
4. Stay away from the hot oil.

**Teachable Moment:** According to lore, barbecued chicken wings were invented in the 1960's in Buffalo, New York (hence the term "buffalo wings") in a small restaurant/bar. Some people had come in for a late night snack and nothing was left but some chicken wings for stock. The customers were so hungry and demanding that the cook reluctantly put the wings under the broiler, covered them in hot sauce, and served them with celery and blue cheese dressing, which were the only other items left in the refrigerator. Hot chicken wings were born.

# Your Shopping List:

- ☐ 1 jar of Louisiana Hot Sauce®
- ☐ 1 package of 24 chicken wings with tips removed (you may substitute chicken drummettes, if desired)
- ☐ 1 16-oz. jar of blue cheese dressing
- ☐ 1 head of celery

## From Your Pantry:

- ☐ margarine, white vinegar, onion powder, garlic, Worcestershire sauce, hot pepper sauce, celery seed powder, red pepper flakes, cayenne pepper, garlic salt, black pepper, vegetable oil for frying, all-purpose flour, paprika

# Beef & Barley Stuffed Peppers

| 3 large | yellow, orange, red and/or green sweet peppers, halved lengthwise and seeded |
|---|---|
| 1 lb. | lean ground beef |
| 1/3 c. | green onions, sliced |
| 1/4 t. | salt |
| 1 c. | barley, cooked |
| 1 c. | prepared chunky salsa |
| 1/3 c. | carrot, grated |
| 1/4 t. | ground cumin |
| 3/4 c. | Jack cheese, shredded |

In a large saucepan, cook the pepper halves in boiling, salted water for 3 to 5 minutes until just tender. Remove from the water and invert the pepper halves over paper towels to drain.

Preheat the oven to 350°F. In a skillet, brown the ground beef and green onions. Season with the salt. Drain off the fat. Stir in the barley, salsa, carrot, and the cumin. Mix well, then add 1/2 cup of cheese and toss. Spoon the barley/beef mixture into the pepper halves and place them into a 9" x 13" baking pan. Bake, covered, in the oven for 20 minutes. Sprinkle the remaining cheese over the peppers and bake, uncovered, for another 5 to 10 minutes. The cheese should be melted when ready to serve. Makes 6 servings.

Kids can help with this recipe:

1. Clean and deseed the peppers.
2. Fill a saucepan with water for the blanching of the peppers.
3. Clean the green onions.
4. Peel the carrot with a child-safe vegetable peeler.
5. Measure the barley, salsa, grated carrot, and cumin. Add to the browned ground beef.
6. Measure 1/2 cup cheese and toss with the barley/beef mixture. Spoon into pepper halves.
7. Sprinkle remaining cheese over the peppers.

**Teachable Moment:** Teach your child helper about peppers. Explain that green bell peppers are the most popular sweet peppers in the United States. As green bell peppers grow and get older, the peppers turn from green to red and get even sweeter! Bell peppers are native to Central and South America and Mexico.

## quick tip

Instead of using barley, you can use other grains you might have leftover from a previous meal. Cooked brown or white rice, bulgur wheat, quinoa, or even couscous can easily substitute for the cooked barley.

## Your Shopping List:

- ❑ 3 large yellow, orange, red and/or green sweet peppers
- ❑ 1 lb. lean ground beef
- ❑ 1/3 bunch of green onions
- ❑ 1 small container of uncooked barley
- ❑ 1 16-oz. jar of prepared chunky salsa
- ❑ 1 medium carrot
- ❑ 1 8-oz. bag of shredded Jack cheese

## From Your Pantry:

- ❑ ground cumin, salt

# Hearty Homemade Chili Con Carne

| | |
|---|---|
| 1 lb. | lean ground beef or turkey |
| 2 cloves | garlic, minced |
| 1 small | white onion, chopped |
| 1 16-oz. | can tomato sauce |
| 1 T. | chili powder |
| 1 t. | salt |
| 1/2 t. | freshly ground black pepper |
| 1 15-oz. | can kidney beans with liquid |
| 1 c. | cheddar cheese, shredded |

In a large saucepan, brown the ground meat and drain any grease. Add the garlic and onion, and cook over medium heat for 1 minute. Add the tomato sauce, chili powder, salt and pepper, and continue cooking for 5 minutes. Add the kidney beans and liquid and cook for 10 minutes, stirring occasionally. Ladle the chili into individual bowls and top with the grated cheese. Makes 4 servings.

Kids can help with this recipe:

1. Older kids can, with supervision, open the cans of tomato sauce and kidney beans with a can opener.

2. Measure the chili powder, salt, and pepper, and add to the browned ground meat mixture. Add the tomato sauce also.

3. Add the kidney beans and liquid.

4. Top the chili with grated cheese.

**Teachable Moment:** Show your child helper the ingredients list on the chili powder bottle. Explain that chili powder actually consists of several spices, typically including dried and powdered onion, garlic, cumin, oregano, pepper, and salt. Chili powder is really a shortcut spice!

# quick tip

You can quickly make this into a full meal by serving the chili over tortilla chips and topping with the shredded cheese, shredded lettuce, and diced tomato. Garnish with a dollop of sour cream and a couple shakes of hot pepper sauce.

# Your Shopping List:

- ❏  1 lb. lean ground beef or turkey
- ❏  1 small white onion
- ❏  1 16-oz. can of tomato sauce
- ❏  1 15-oz. can of kidney beans
- ❏  1 8-oz. bag of shredded cheddar cheese

## From Your Pantry:
- ❏  garlic, chili powder, salt, black pepper

# Cheese-Crusted Chicken Pot Pie

| | |
|---|---|
| 1 10-3/4 oz. | can cream of chicken soup |
| 1/2 c. | milk or cream |
| 1 t. | salt |
| 1/2 t. | black pepper |
| 1-1/2 c. | cooked chicken, cut into small cubes |
| 1 10-oz. | pkg. frozen mixed vegetables (carrots, peas, beans, etc.) |

**Cheese Crust:**

| | |
|---|---|
| 1 c. | prepared baking mix |
| 1/2 c. | milk |
| 1 | egg |
| 1/2 c. | cheddar cheese, shredded |

Preheat the oven to 350°F. In a deep-dish pie pan or casserole dish, mix together the soup, milk or cream, salt, pepper, chicken, and vegetables. Smooth the top evenly. Prepare the Cheese Crust by combining the baking mix, milk, egg and shredded cheese in a medium bowl. Gently spoon the crust over the chicken and vegetables and smooth the top evenly again. Bake the pie for 30 to 40 minutes or until the pie is heated through and the crust is golden brown. Makes 4 servings.

Kids can help with this recipe:

1. Older kids can, with supervision, open the can of soup with a can opener.

2. Measure the milk or cream, salt, and black pepper. Add to the chicken and vegetables in the baking dish.

3. Measure the ingredients for the Cheese Crust and combine.

# Your Shopping List:

- ☐ 1 10-3/4 oz. can of cream of chicken soup
- ☐ 1-1/2 c. cooked chicken
- ☐ 1 10-oz. package of frozen mixed vegetables (carrots, peas, beans, etc.)
- ☐ 1 egg
- ☐ 1 8-oz. bag of shredded cheddar cheese

## From Your Pantry:

- ☐ milk or cream, salt, black pepper, prepared baking mix

## quick tip

This casserole can be prepared the night before. Just make the filling and cheese crust, cover in plastic wrap, and refrigerate. When you come home the next day, remove the plastic wrap, pop the casserole in a pre-heated oven, and throw together a quick salad. Dinner will be ready in 30 to 40 minutes. How easy is that?

# Slow-Cooked Wild Mushroom Chicken

| | |
|---|---|
| 1 T. | butter |
| 1 small | white onion, finely chopped |
| 2 c. | fresh mushroom varieties (such as crimini, oyster, chanterelle, shiitake), thinly sliced |
| 1/4 t. | salt |
| 1 t. | fresh thyme, minced |
| 3 to 4 lbs. | fryer chicken, cut into pieces |
| 1 t. | salt |
| 1 t. | freshly ground black pepper |
| 1/4 t. | ground paprika |
| 1 1-1/2 oz. | pkg. dehydrated onion soup mix |
| 1 10-3/4 oz. | can cream of mushroom soup |
| 1/4 c. | low fat milk |

In a large skillet, melt the butter over medium heat. When foamy, add the white onion, mushroom slices, 1/4 t. salt, and fresh thyme. Sauté over medium high heat until the mushrooms are soft and all of their liquid has evaporated. Turn off the heat and set aside.

Place the chicken in a large ovenproof casserole dish and dust each piece with the salt, pepper, and paprika. Mix together the onion soup, mushroom soup, milk and sautéed mushrooms, and pour the mix over the chicken. Bake at 350°F for 2 hours or until the chicken is very tender. Makes 4 servings.

Kids can help with this recipe:

1. Clean the mushrooms with a damp towel.
2. Measure and add the butter to the skillet.
3. Measure the salt and thyme and season the mushrooms.
4. Place the chicken pieces in the casserole dish.
5. Measure the salt, black pepper, and paprika, and season the chicken.
6. Older kids, with supervision, can open the can of soup with a can opener.
7. Measure the milk and mix with the onion soup, mushroom soup, and milk.
8. Pour the soup mixture over the chicken.

**Teachable Moment:** This is a good opportunity to talk about mushrooms with your child helper. Mushrooms are members of the fungi family, so they are technically not vegetables. Mushrooms can be cultivated, including white button, crimini, and portabello mushrooms. Wild mushrooms, such as chanterelles, boletes, and morels, are tasty but should only be picked by experienced mushroom hunters. Never eat a mushroom that you have found outside!

# Your Shopping List:

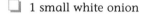

- ☐ 1 small white onion
- ☐ 2 c. fresh mushroom varieties (such as crimini, oyster, chanterelle, shiitake)
- ☐ 3 to 4 lbs. fryer chicken
- ☐ 1 10-3/4 oz. can of cream of mushroom soup

## From Your Pantry:

- ☐ salt, black pepper, paprika, low fat milk

**quick tip**

If you're pressed for time, you can used 2 4-oz. cans of sliced mushrooms, drained, instead of sautéing the fresh mushrooms and onion. You can also simmer boneless, skinless chicken breasts in the sauce until cooked through in place of slow-cooking the chicken pieces.

# Game Day Baked Beans

| | |
|---|---|
| 1 16-oz. | can baked beans |
| 1/4 c. | onion, chopped |
| 1/4 c. | brown sugar |
| 2 T. | honey |
| 2 t. | Dijon mustard |
| 1/2 c. | ketchup |
| 1/2 t. | salt |
| 4 slices | bacon, uncooked |

Preheat the oven to 350°F. Grease an ovenproof pan or Dutch oven. Combine the beans, onion, brown sugar, and honey, and mix lightly. Add the mustard, ketchup, and salt, and mix again. Place the slices of bacon over the top of the beans and bake uncovered for 30 to 40 minutes or until the bacon is cooked crisp and the beans are heated throughout. Makes 6 servings.

Kids can help with this recipe:

1. Older kids can, with supervision, open the can of beans with a can opener.
2. Measure the chopped onion, brown sugar, honey, mustard, ketchup, and salt. Add to the beans and combine.
3. Place the bacon slices on top of the beans.

**Teachable Moment:** Ketchup is considered America's favorite condiment. Over 97% of US households have a bottle of ketchup. Ketchup was first imported to Europe from China (it was called "ketsiap") in the 1600's, but it did not contain tomatoes. Tomato-based ketchup was first produced in the 1800's.

# Your Shopping List:

- ☐ 1 16-oz. can of baked beans
- ☐ 1 small white onion
- ☐ 4 slices of bacon, uncooked

## From Your Pantry:

- ☐ brown sugar, honey, Dijon mustard, ketchup, salt

## quick tip

You can easily double or even triple this recipe for large crowds or for another meal later in the week. Serve this crowd-pleaser with cornbread and a green salad.

# Crispy Parmesan Fried Chicken

| | |
|---|---|
| 4 | boneless, skinless chicken breasts |
| 1 | egg, beaten |
| 1 c. | flour |
| 1 t. | black pepper |
| 1/2 c. | Parmesan cheese, grated |
| 2 T. | vegetable oil |

Pound the chicken breasts until thin. Place the egg in a shallow dish. Mix together in a plastic bag the flour, pepper, and Parmesan cheese. Heat the oil in a large frying pan until hot. Dip each piece of chicken in the egg and then in the flour/cheese coating. Press as much coating as possible onto each piece. Fry the chicken breasts in the pan for 5 minutes, uncovered. Turn and fry for 3 to 5 minutes or until the juices run clear. Makes 4 servings.

Kids can help with this recipe:

1. Crack open and beat the egg.
2. Measure the oil and place in the unheated frying pan.
3. Measure the flour, black pepper, and Parmesan cheese. Place in a plastic bag and combine.
4. Dip the chicken in the egg and then in the flour/cheese coating.

# Your Shopping List:

- ❑ 4 boneless, skinless chicken breasts
- ❑ 1 egg
- ❑ 1 8-oz. container of freshly grated Parmesan cheese

## From Your Pantry:

- ❑ flour, black pepper, vegetable oil

## quick tip

You can also use Italian-seasoned bread-crumbs instead of the flour and black pepper. The Italian seasoning will add extra flavor to this dish. Or, you can add your own Italian seasoning to the flour and black pepper. Serve with marinara sauce on the side.

# Hearty Chicken & Biscuits

| | |
|---|---|
| 6 c. | cooked chicken, cut into small pieces |
| 1 c. | onion, chopped |
| 1 c. | celery, chopped |
| 1 c. | red bell pepper, chopped |
| 1 c. | broccoli florets, chopped |
| 1 c. | carrots, peeled and cubed |
| 2 14-1/2 oz. | cans chicken broth |
| 1/3 c. | cornstarch |
| 3/4 c. | water |
| 4 c. | prepared baking mix |
| 1-1/2 c. | milk |
| 2 T. | sugar |
| 1 T. | fresh parsley, minced |

Using a large saucepan, heat the chicken, onion, celery, red bell pepper, broccoli, carrots, and chicken broth to boiling. In a small bowl, mix the cornstarch with the water until smooth and slowly add to the boiling broth. Stir until the mixture boils again and the broth is thickened. Boil 1 minute. Remove from the heat and pour the chicken and vegetables into a 9" x 13" baking pan.

Combine the baking mix, milk, sugar and parsley in a medium bowl and mix until no lumps remain. Using a soupspoon, drop biscuits the size of large walnuts over the chicken and vegetables, covering the top of the baking pan completely. Bake, uncovered, at 400°F for 25 to 30 minutes, or until the biscuits are cooked through. Makes 6 servings.

Kids can help with this recipe:

1. Older kids can, with supervision, open the cans of chicken broth with a can opener.
2. Wash the vegetables. Deseed the red pepper.
3. Peel the carrot with a child-safe vegetable peeler.
4. Measure the chicken chunks, chopped onion, celery, red pepper, broccoli, and carrots. Add to a large saucepan along with the chicken broth.
5. Measure the cornstarch and water and mix together in small bowl until smooth.
6. Measure and combine the baking mix, milk, sugar, and parsley in a medium bowl.

**Teachable Moment:** Broccoli is considered a "super vegetable" because it is chock full of wonderful vitamins and nutrients. Broccoli can be boiled, steamed, baked, fried, and eaten raw. The word "broccoli" comes from the Italian word "brocco," which means branch or arm. The average American eats 4-1/2 pounds of broccoli a year!

# Your Shopping List:

- ❑ 6 c. cooked chicken (about 2-1/2 lbs.)
- ❑ 1 medium yellow onion
- ❑ 2 celery stalks
- ❑ 1 large red pepper
- ❑ 1 bag of pre-washed broccoli florets
- ❑ 1 large carrot
- ❑ 2 14-1/2 oz. cans of chicken broth
- ❑ 1 bunch of fresh Italian flat-leaf parsley

# From Your Pantry:

- ❑ cornstarch, prepared baking mix, milk, sugar

**quick tip**

If you're really pressed for time, you can use frozen vegetables for this recipe to avoid the step of preparing the vegetables. Also, use leftover chicken from a previous meal or use a slow cooker to prepare the meat from a stewing chicken during the day. Or, you can simply pick up a rotisserie chicken from your supermarket.

# Foil-Wrapped Roast Beef

| | |
|---|---|
| 3 lbs. | beef chuck roast |
| 3 large | russet potatoes, cut into quarters |
| 3 large | carrots, peeled and cut into 2-inch pieces |
| 1 large | onion, peeled and cut into quarters |
| 1 1-1/2 oz. | pkg. dry onion soup mix |
| 1 10-3/4 oz. | can cream of mushroom soup |
| 2 T. | water |

Cut 2 large pieces of aluminum foil to overlap a 9" x 13" baking pan. Tightly seal any cut edges in the pan. Place the roast in the middle of the foil. Add the potatoes, carrots, and onion around and on top of the roast. In a small bowl, mix together the onion soup mix and cream of mushroom soup. Spoon the sauce over the roast and vegetables, and sprinkle the water over all. Cut two pieces of aluminum foil and tightly seal the top of the roast and vegetables, tucking and sealing in all of the edges. Bake at 325°F for 3 hours or until the meat and vegetables are very tender. Serve, spooning the gravy over the meat and vegetables. Makes 4 to 6 servings.

Kids can help with this recipe:

1. Clean the vegetables.
2. Peel the carrots with a child-safe vegetable peeler.
3. Place the vegetables around and on top of the roast.
4. Older kids can, with supervision, open the soup can with a can opener.
5. Combine the onion soup and cream of mushroom soup in a small bowl. Spoon over the roast.
6. Measure the water.

# Your Shopping List:

- ❑ 3 lbs. beef chuck roast
- ❑ 3 large russet potatoes
- ❑ 3 large carrots
- ❑ 1 large onion
- ❑ 1 10-3/4 oz. can of cream of mushroom soup

## From Your Pantry:
- ❑ dry onion soup mix, aluminum foil

# quick tip

Rather than cutting the aluminum foil, you can also buy an aluminum foil bag that will work just as well. These foil bags are the perfect medium in which to roast meats, poultry, and fish. They seal in the flavor and make clean up easy.

## Pork Chops in Midnight Marinade

| | |
|---|---|
| 3 T. | Worcestershire sauce |
| 1/2 c. | dry white wine |
| 2 T. | extra-virgin olive oil |
| 1 t. | salt |
| 1 t. | freshly ground black pepper |
| 2 t. | hot chili sauce |
| 1 T. | apple cider vinegar |
| 3 T. | soy sauce |
| 1/4 c. | dark brown sugar |
| 4 | pork loin chops, 6 to 8 ounces each |

Combine all of the ingredients except for the pork chops in a large, self-sealing plastic bag. Mix thoroughly. Add the pork chops and marinate in the refrigerator for 2 hours or up to 12 hours. Remove the chops from the bag and discard the marinade. Grill the chops over medium coals for 5 to 6 minutes. Turn and grill for 4 to 5 minutes longer, or until cooked to your preference. Makes 4 servings.

Kids can help with this recipe:

1. Measure all of the ingredients (except the pork) and place in large, resealable plastic bag. Mix to combine.

2. Add the pork chops to the bag.

## Your Shopping List:

❑ 4 pork loin chops, 6 to 8 ounces each

### From Your Pantry:

❑ Worcestershire sauce, dry white wine, extra-virgin olive oil, salt, black pepper, hot chili sauce, apple cider vinegar, soy sauce, dark brown sugar

## quick tip

This recipe can be prepared the night before for an easy entrée the next day. You can also use the Midnight Marinade on other cuts of pork. Serve with rice and vegetables for a tasty meal.

# Creamy Tuna with Noodles

| | |
|---|---|
| 1 12-1/2 oz. | can tuna, drained |
| 1 10-3/4 oz. | can condensed cream of mushroom soup |
| 1/4 c. | milk |
| 1 t. | black pepper |
| 1/4 c. | onions, chopped |
| 1 12-oz. | pkg. egg noodles, cooked al dente |
| 2 c. | crushed potato chips |

In a large mixing bowl, combine the tuna, soup, milk, pepper, and onions. Add the noodles and mix well. Lightly coat an 8" x 8" baking pan with cooking spray and pour the tuna/noodle mixture into the pan. Top with the crushed potato chips and bake at 350°F for 30 to 35 minutes. Makes 4 to 6 servings.

Kids can help with this recipe:

1. Fill a stockpot with water to cook the noodles.

2. Apply cooking spray to the baking pan.

3. Older kids can, with supervision, open the cans of tuna and soup with a can opener.

4. Measure the milk, black pepper, and onions. Combine in a large mixing bowl with the tuna and soup.

5. Measure and crush the potato chips. Sprinkle over the uncooked casserole.

**Teachable Moment:** Americans eat 1.2 billion pounds of potato chips a year!

# Your Shopping List:

- ☐ 1 12-1/2 oz. can of tuna
- ☐ 1 10-3/4 oz. condensed cream of mushroom soup
- ☐ 1 small white onion
- ☐ 1 12-oz. package of egg noodles
- ☐ 1 medium bag of potato chips

## From Your Pantry:

- ☐ milk, black pepper, cooking spray

## quick tip

You can prepare this dish the night before and refrigerate. Top with potato chips just before placing the casserole in the oven. You can also substitute canned salmon for the tuna.

# Stockpot Chicken with Spring Vegetables

| | |
|---|---|
| 4 | chicken breast halves, skinless and boneless |
| 1 T. | extra-virgin olive oil |
| 1 | yellow onion, chopped |
| 1 c. | whole baby carrots |
| 1 15-oz. | can diced tomatoes, undrained |
| 2 cloves | garlic, minced |
| 1 t. | salt |
| 1/2 t. | black pepper |
| 1/2 t. | chili powder |
| 1 15-oz. | can whole new potatoes, cut in half |
| 1 10-oz. | pkg. frozen green beans |
| 1 c. | canned or frozen whole kernel corn |

Chop the chicken into small chunks. In a large stockpot, brown the chicken in the olive oil over medium heat for 2 minutes. Turn and brown again. Reduce the heat and add the onion, carrots, tomatoes, salt, pepper, and chili powder. Stir well and simmer for 8 minutes. Add the new potatoes, green beans, and corn and stir again. Simmer for 5 to 8 minutes or until the soup is heated through and the vegetables are tender-crisp. Makes 4 servings.

Kids can help with this recipe:

1. Measure the olive oil and place in an unheated stockpot.
2. Mince the garlic with a garlic press.
3. Older kids can, with supervision, open the cans of tomato and potato with a can opener.
4. Measure the baby carrots, salt, black pepper, and chili powder. Add to the chicken, along with the onion, carrots, and tomato.
5. Measure the corn.
6. Add the new potatoes, green beans, and corn.

# Your Shopping List:

- ❑ 4 chicken breast halves, skinless and boneless
- ❑ 1 medium yellow onion
- ❑ 1 small bag of whole baby carrots
- ❑ 1 15-oz. can of diced tomatoes
- ❑ 1 15-oz. can of whole new potatoes, cut in half
- ❑ 1 10-oz. package of frozen green beans
- ❑ 1 16-oz. package of frozen whole kernel corn

## From Your Pantry:

- ❑ Extra-virgin olive oil, garlic, salt, black pepper, chili powder

## quick tip

We included canned and frozen vegetables to speed up the cooking process of this dish. However, you could easily use fresh new potatoes, green beans, and corn and alter the cooking time accordingly. You could also use any other leftover vegetables you might have in your refrigerator.

# Spicy Cheese & Potato Soup

| | |
|---|---|
| 2 10-3/4 oz. | cans condensed cheddar cheese soup |
| 1 c. | cream |
| 1 c. | milk |
| 4 medium | red jacket potatoes, roughly chopped |
| 1 8-oz. | can corn kernels, drained or 1 cup frozen corn kernels |
| 1 7-oz. | can diced green chilies |
| 2 | green onions, thinly sliced |
| 1/2 t. | salt |
| 1/2 t. | black pepper |
| 1/4 t. | chili powder |

Combine the cans of soup, cream and milk in a large saucepan. Cook on medium heat, stirring to blend. Add the potatoes, bring to a boil, and simmer for 5 to 7 minutes. Add the corn and diced green chilies. Heat for 2 minutes. Add the salt, pepper, and chili powder and stir well. Simmer for 10 minutes. Makes 4 servings.

Kids can help with this recipe:

1. Older kids can, with supervision, open the cans of soup and corn with a can opener.
2. Measure the cream and milk and add to the cans of soup in the saucepan.
3. Add the corn.

# Your Shopping List:

- ❏ 2 10-3/4 oz. cans of condensed cheddar cheese soup
- ❏ 1 half-pint cream
- ❏ 1 8-oz. can of corn kernels or 1 bag of frozen corn kernels
- ❏ 4 medium red jacket potatoes
- ❏ 1 7-oz. can of diced green chilies
- ❏ 1 bunch of green onions

## From Your Pantry:

- ❏ milk, salt, black pepper, chili powder

## quick tip

Instead of using diced green chilies and plain corn, substitute a can of Mexican corn, which you can find in the Latino section of your grocery store. You can also speed up cooking time by using canned new potatoes instead of fresh potatoes.

# Quick Oven Cinnamon & Butter Pancake

| | |
|---|---|
| 1/2 c. | all-purpose flour |
| 3 | eggs, lightly beaten |
| 1/2 c. | whole milk |
| 2 T. | butter, melted |
| 1/4 t. | salt |
| 1/2 t. | ground cinnamon |
| | powdered sugar for dusting |
| | maple syrup on the side |

Preheat the oven to 450°F. Grease a 10-inch ovenproof skillet. Sift the flour. In a medium bowl, lightly beat the eggs. Gradually whisk the flour into the eggs. Stir in the milk, butter, salt, and cinnamon. Pour the batter into the prepared skillet. Bake for 20 minutes. Remove the skillet from the heat. Cut the pancake into 6 wedges and dust with powdered sugar. Serve immediately with maple syrup on the side. Makes 6 servings.

Kids can help with this recipe:

1. Measure and sift the flour.
2. Crack open and beat the eggs.
3. Measure the butter and melt in the microwave (with supervision).
4. Measure the milk, salt, and cinnamon. Add to the flour mixture along with the melted butter, and stir to combine.
5. Dust powdered sugar on the pancake wedges.

## quick tip

If you have slightly stale sliced bread, you can alter this recipe to make French toast. Just omit the flour and combine the remaining ingredients together. Soak the bread slices in the egg batter and fry in a nonstick skillet, turning over once. Serve with powdered sugar and maple syrup. Enjoy!

**Teachable Moment:** Cinnamon is a spice that comes from the dried bark of an Asian evergreen tree, native to Sri Lanka. Let your child helper see both the ground and stick forms of cinnamon. Explain that cinnamon was such a prized spice in ancient times that it was considered a gift fit for a king or queen. In fact, the search for cinnamon and other ancient spices led the Europeans to explore new lands.

# Your Shopping List:

❑  3 eggs

# From Your Pantry:

❑  flour, milk, butter, salt, ground cinnamon, powdered sugar, maple syrup

# Summer Ambrosia Fruit Salad

| | |
|---|---|
| 1 | apple, peeled and chopped |
| 2 | ripe bananas, peeled and sliced |
| 1 | fresh peach, peeled, pitted, and chopped |
| 1 | small basket of strawberries, hulled and quartered |
| 1 8-oz. | can pineapple chunks, drained |
| 1/2 t. | ground cinnamon |
| 1/2 c. | walnuts, chopped |
| 1 c. | prepared whipped cream |

In a large bowl combine the apple, bananas, peaches, strawberries, pineapple, and walnuts. Sprinkle the fruit with the cinnamon and toss. Gently fold in the whipped cream. Serve immediately. Makes 6 servings.

Kids can help with this recipe:

1. Wash and dry the apple, peach, and strawberries.
2. Peel and slice the bananas with a butter knife.
3. Older kids can, with supervision, open the can of pineapple chunks with a can opener, and drain.
4. Measure the walnuts.
5. Combine the prepared fruit and walnuts in a mixing bowl.
6. Measure the prepared whipped cream.

**Teachable Moment:** Your child helper would be interested to learn that "ambrosia" was considered the food of the Greek gods. Ancient Greek myth states that Apollo, son of Zeus and symbol of the Sun, was raised on ambrosia. Ambrosia is now associated with sweetness.

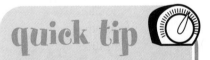

## quick tip

This is a fantastic way to use up any extra fruit. In addition to the fruit listed in the ingredients above, you could use grapes, pears, nectarines, mandarin oranges, pitted cherries, mango, papaya, kiwi, berries, and any drained canned fruit. You can also use non-dairy whipped topping.

# Your Shopping List:

- ☐ 1 large apple
- ☐ 2 ripe bananas
- ☐ 1 large fresh peach
- ☐ 1 small basket of strawberries
- ☐ 1 8-oz. can of pineapple chunks
- ☐ 1 3-oz. bag of chopped walnuts
- ☐ 1 8-oz. container of prepared whipped cream

## From Your Pantry:

- ☐ ground cinnamon

# French Three-Onion Soup

| | |
|---|---|
| 1 T. | extra-virgin olive oil |
| 4 large | Vidalia onions, peeled and sliced into 1/4-inch rounds |
| 1 bunch | green onions, white parts only, thinly sliced |
| 4 large | shallots, peeled and chopped |
| 2 c. | beef broth |
| dash | salt |
| 1/4 t. | ground black pepper |
| 4 slices | French bread, toasted |
| 1/2 c. | Gruyère cheese, grated |
| 2 T. | fresh chives, chopped |

In a large skillet over medium heat, heat the olive oil. Add the onions, green onions, and the shallots and stir. Reduce the heat to low and cook the onions slowly for 20 minutes until they are caramelized, stirring occasionally. If the onions become too dry, add a little water to prevent burning.

Preheat the broiler. Add the beef broth to the onions and simmer for an additional 15 minutes. Season with the salt and pepper. Ladle the soup into four ovenproof individual bowls. Top each bowl of soup with a slice of toasted French bread and sprinkle mozzarella cheese over each piece of bread. Place the bowls on a sturdy baking sheet and put the bowls 3 inches from the broiler to melt the cheese. Top the melted cheese with a sprinkling of chives. Makes 4 servings.

Kids can help with this recipe:

1. Measure the olive oil and place in an unheated skillet.
2. Grate the cheese.
3. Older kids can, with supervision, open the can of beef broth with a can opener.
4. Add the beef broth to the cooked onions.
5. Measure salt and pepper and season.
6. Top each bowl with a slice of toasted French bread and sprinkle with cheese.
7. Top with chives.

**Teachable Moment:** Because this recipe uses 3 different kinds of onions, it offers a great moment to teach your child helper about onions. Explain that onions are one of the oldest cultivated vegetables. Ancient Egyptian leaders would take an oath of office with their right hand on an onion. Onions come in many different forms and colors from white and yellow to red and purple. They also vary in sweetness and flavor. Onions are used throughout the world.

# Your Shopping List:

- 4 large Vidalia onions
- 1 bunch of green onions
- 4 large shallots
- 2 14-oz. cans of beef broth
- 1 demi-loaf of French bread
- 4 oz. Gruyère cheese
- 1 bunch of fresh chives

## From Your Pantry:

- extra-virgin olive oil, salt, black pepper

## quick tip

You can substitute the shallots and green onions with another Vidalia onion. You can also substitute the Gruyère cheese with Monterey Jack or mozzarella cheese.

# It Only Takes A Healthy Note

**5**

One of the reasons why you cook at home is to be assured that you and your family are eating healthfully. As you know, many studies have shown that home-cooking is simply healthier than consuming restaurant food. You have absolute control over the ingredients in whatever you make and you can alter a recipe to reflect your personal taste or dietary restrictions. You can use the best quality ingredients and the freshest produce and meat.

This chapter gives you recipes that are all low in fat and calories. But, unlike many other "healthy" recipes that are blah in flavor, these dishes are chock full of delicious goodness. And, most importantly, they are easy to make and require minimal preparation time. Your family will not even know they are eating health food; they will be focusing only on the scrumptious flavors bursting on their palates!

By the end of this chapter, you will:

- make healthy but delicious food with a minimal amount of effort
- learn which non-fat ingredients can be used to create tasty dishes
- discover that fresh herbs and seasonings can pump up the flavor of food without adding fat
- know which recipes can be prepared in advance or made with a slow cooker
- teach your child helper some fascinating food history

- allow your child helpers to gain more independence by teaching them food preparation skills
- use our handy lists to streamline your grocery shopping
- utilize your pantry to minimize shopping
- add healthy, tasty recipes to your repertoire of quick cooking

# Lemon Petrale Fillet of Sole

| 2 T. | white vinegar |
|------|---------------|
| 1 T. | fresh lemon juice |
| 1/4 c. | extra-virgin olive oil |
| 2 t. | salt |
| 1 t. | garlic powder |
| 1 t. | freshly ground black pepper |
| 1 t. | dry mustard |
| 4 8 oz. | petrale sole fillets |
| | lemon wedges for garnish |

Prepare the marinade by combining all of the ingredients except the sole fillets and lemon wedges. Place the fillets in a large glass pan and cover with the marinade. Cover tightly with plastic wrap and refrigerate for 1 hour or up to 2 hours. Turn once while marinating.

Lightly oil your barbecue grids. Grill the fish over medium coals for 4 to 5 minutes. Turn and grill for 4 to 5 minutes more or until the fish flakes easily. Serve with lemon wedges. Makes 4 servings.

| Calories: | 336 |
|-----------|-----|
| Total Fat: | 17g |
| Saturated Fat: | 3g |
| % Calories from Fat: | 46 |
| Carbohydrates: | 1g |
| Protein: | 43g |
| Cholesterol: | 109mg |
| Sodium: | 767mg |

Kids can help with this recipe:

1. Squeeze 1 lemon for its juice. Remove any seeds.
2. Measure the white vinegar, lemon juice, olive oil, salt, garlic powder, black pepper, and dry mustard. Mix well to form a marinade.
3. Place the fish fillets in a glass pan and pour the marinade on top.

**Teachable Moment:** This is a great opportunity to teach your child helper about different kinds of fish, pointing out that the sole is especially unusual. The sole is a flatfish that spends most of its life lying on the bottom of the ocean floor, covered in sand and mud. Its left eye actually moves to the right side of its head as it gets older. It also can change the color of its skin to match its environment!

## Your Shopping List:

❑  3 ripe lemons (for juice and as garnish)
❑  4 petrale sole fillets, about 8 ounces each

### From Your Pantry:

❑  white vinegar, extra-virgin olive oil, salt, garlic powder, black pepper, dry mustard

**quick tip**

You can buy a bottle of prepared lemon vinaigrette and use in place of the marinade.

# Scallops with a Parmesan Crust

| | |
|---|---|
| 1/2 c. | seasoned bread crumbs |
| 1/4 t. | garlic powder |
| 1/4 c. | low fat shredded Parmesan cheese |
| 1/4 t. | dry mustard |
| 1/4 t. | onion powder |
| 1 lb. | sea scallops, rinsed |
| 1/2 c. | fat-free plain yogurt |

Preheat oven to 450°F. Line a baking sheet with aluminum foil and then spray the foil with cooking spray. In a small bowl, combine the breadcrumbs, garlic powder, Parmesan cheese, dry mustard, and the onion powder. Mix well and pour onto a plate. Dip the sea scallops into the yogurt and then roll them in the breadcrumb mix. Coat the scallops completely. Arrange the scallops on the baking sheet. Lightly spray the prepared scallops with cooking spray and bake for 10 to 15 minutes until golden brown. Makes 4 servings.

| | |
|---|---|
| Calories: | 187 |
| Total Fat: | 3g |
| Saturated Fat: | <1g |
| % Calories from Fat: | 13 |
| Carbohydrates: | 16g |
| Protein: | 23g |
| Cholesterol: | 40mg |
| Sodium: | 541mg |

## quick tip

Make sure to get dry-packed sea scallops at your market's seafood department. These scallops are extra fresh and do not have any chemical preservatives added to them, as wet scallops do. Also, because they have been dry-packed, these scallops will cook faster and will brown even better than the wet scallops.

Kids can help with this recipe:

1. Apply cooking spray to foil-covered baking sheet.
2. Measure the breadcrumbs, garlic powder, cheese, dry mustard, and onion powder. Mix to combine.
3. Measure the yogurt and dip the scallops into it.
4. Roll the scallops in the breadcrumb mix and place on the baking sheet.
5. Lightly spray the scallops with cooking spray.

## Your Shopping List:

- ☐ 1 10-oz. container of seasoned breadcrumbs
- ☐ 1 8-oz. container of low fat shredded Parmesan cheese
- ☐ 1 lb. fresh sea scallops
- ☐ 1 8-oz. container of fat-free plain yogurt

## From Your Pantry:

- ☐ garlic powder, dry mustard, onion powder, aluminum foil, cooking spray

# Herbed Halibut Fillets

| | |
|---|---|
| 2 | halibut fillets, about 1-inch thick |
| 4 T. | fat-free sour cream |
| 2 t. | lemon juice |
| 1-1/2 t. | dry ranch dressing mix |
| 1/8 t. | ground black pepper |

In a small bowl, combine the sour cream, lemon juice, ranch dressing mix, and the black pepper. Stir until well blended. Place the halibut fillets on a broiler pan. Cover each fillet with the sour cream sauce. Broil 8 to 10 minutes. The fillets will be done when they easily flake with a fork. Makes 2 servings.

| | |
|---|---|
| Calories: | 240 |
| Total Fat: | 6g |
| Saturated Fat: | <1g |
| % Calories from Fat: | 22 |
| Carbohydrates: | 7g |
| Protein: | 38g |
| Cholesterol: | 60mg |
| Sodium: | 151mg |

Kids can help with this recipe:

1. Squeeze the lemon for its juice. Remove any seeds.
2. Measure the sour cream, lemon juice, ranch dressing mix, and black pepper. Combine and stir until well blended.

# Your Shopping List:

- ☐ 2 halibut fillets, about 1 inch thick
- ☐ 1 8-oz. container of fat-free sour cream
- ☐ 1 fresh lemon, for its juice
- ☐ 1 1-oz. packet of dry ranch dressing mix

## From Your Pantry:

- ☐ black pepper

## quick tip

You can substitute any white-fleshed fish fillets for the halibut. You can also make your own ranch dressing mix by combining dried dill, dried parsley, onion powder, garlic powder, and salt to taste. You can also add in any of your favorite dried herbs.

# Turkey Stroganoff

| | |
|---|---|
| 1-1/2 lb. | ground turkey |
| 1/2 c. | yellow onion, thinly sliced |
| 1 clove | garlic, minced |
| 1/2 t. | seasoned salt |
| 1/4 t. | ground black pepper |
| 1/2 c. | crimini mushrooms, sliced |
| 1-1/2 c. | low sodium, fat-free chicken broth |
| 3 T. | tomato paste |
| 1 c. | water |
| 3 T. | flour |
| 12 oz. | yolk-free noodles, cooked and drained |

Spray a large skillet with cooking spray. Cook the ground turkey, onion, garlic, seasoned salt, black pepper, and the sliced mushrooms over medium high heat until the meat is browned. Stir in the chicken broth and the tomato paste. Bring to a boil over high heat. In a small bowl, combine 1 cup of water with the 3 tablespoons of flour until it is well blended. Add to the turkey mixture and stir until the sauce thickens. Reduce the heat to low; cover and simmer for 45 minutes. Serve over the hot, cooked noodles. Makes 6 servings.

| | |
|---|---|
| Calories: | 447 |
| Total Fat: | 15g |
| Saturated Fat: | 3g |
| % Calories from Fat: | 27 |
| Carbohydrates: | 54g |
| Protein: | 34g |
| Cholesterol: | 90mg |
| Sodium: | 336mg |

Kids can help with this recipe:

1. Fill an unheated stockpot with water to cook the noodles.

2. Apply cooking spray to a large skillet.

3. Mince the garlic in a garlic press.

4. Measure the yellow onion, seasoned salt, black pepper, and sliced mushrooms, and add to the skillet with the ground turkey and garlic.

5. Older kids can, with supervision, open the cans of chicken broth and tomato paste with a can opener.

6. Measure the chicken broth and tomato paste and add to the skillet.

7. Measure and combine water and flour. Stir until well blended.

8. Carefully add flour mixture to the dish, avoiding the hot skillet.

**Teachable Moment:** Your child helper might be fascinated to know that the original beef stroganoff dish was named after a 19th century Russian diplomat, Count Pavel Stroganov. Created by the Count's chef, it was the winning dish in a cooking competition in St. Petersburg, Russia.

# Your Shopping List:

- ☐ 1-1/2 lb. ground turkey
- ☐ 1 medium yellow onion
- ☐ 6 small crimini mushrooms
- ☐ 1 14-oz. can of low sodium, fat-free chicken broth
- ☐ 1 6-oz. can of tomato paste (or 1 tube of tomato paste)
- ☐ 1 12-oz. package of yolk-free noodles

## From Your Pantry:

- ☐ garlic, seasoned salt, black pepper, flour, cooking spray

# quick tip

Buying tomato paste in a tube ultimately saves you time and money. These tomato paste tubes are small, reusable, and easily stored in the refrigerator. Because most recipes that call for tomato paste only require a small amount, opening a whole can of tomato paste can prove wasteful. If you do choose to save the remaining tomato paste from the can, you have to place it in a resealable plastic container to be stored in the refrigerator, which takes time and valuable refrigerator space.

# Hot Caribbean Beans and Rice

| | |
|---|---|
| 2/3 c. | instant white rice, uncooked |
| 1/3 c. + 1 T. | fat-free chicken broth |
| 1/3 c. | water |
| 1 c. | white onion, chopped |
| 1/2 c. | celery, chopped |
| 1/2 c. | green bell pepper, chopped |
| 1-1/2 t. | garlic, minced |
| 1 c. | canned chopped tomatoes, drained |
| 1/4 t. | ground cumin |
| 1/4 t. | crushed red pepper flakes |
| 1 t. | Worcestershire sauce |
| 1 15 oz. | can black beans, rinsed and drained |
| 2 T. | fresh cilantro, chopped |

Cook the rice according to the package directions using 1/3 cup of chicken broth and 1/3 cup of water. Set aside and keep warm. Spray a large skillet with cooking spray. Place 1 tablespoon of the chicken broth in the skillet and heat over medium high heat. Add the onion, celery, green pepper, and the garlic and cook, stirring frequently, until the vegetables are just tender. Add the tomatoes, cumin, crushed red pepper, and the Worcestershire sauce and cook for 2 to 3 minutes. Stir in the cooked rice, beans, and the cilantro. Stir to combine well and cook for 5 to 6 minutes or until heated through. Makes 4 servings.

| | |
|---|---|
| Calories: | 235 |
| Total Fat: | 1g |
| Saturated Fat: | <1g |
| % Calories from Fat: | 4 |
| Carbohydrates: | 50g |
| Protein: | 10g |
| Cholesterol: | 0mg |
| Sodium: | 501mg |

Kids can help with this recipe:

1. Older kids can, with supervision, open the can of chicken broth with a can opener.

2. Measure the rice, chicken broth, and water for cooking the rice.

3. Apply cooking spray to a large skillet.

## quick tip

For added flavor and ease, you can substitute an 8 oz. package of chicken-flavored instant rice for the plain instant rice, chicken broth, and water. Cook and add to the recipe as indicated.

4. Clean the vegetables and cilantro and deseed the green pepper.

5. Measure 1 T. chicken broth and place in the skillet.

6. Mince the garlic with a garlic press.

7. Measure the onion, celery, green pepper, and add to the skillet along with the garlic.

8. Older kids can, with supervision, open the cans of tomatoes and beans with a can opener.

9. Measure the tomatoes, cumin, crushed red pepper, and Worcestershire sauce and add to the skillet.

**Teachable Moment:** Cooking can also be a way to teach a child about geography. This is the perfect dish in this regard. Show your child helper where the Caribbean is on a map and talk to them about all the ethnic influences there: French, African, Dutch, American Indian, British, Spanish, etc. Explain that many Caribbean dishes, like American dishes, are a combination of various ethnic traditions and foods.

# Your Shopping List:

- ☐ 1 14-oz. package of instant white rice
- ☐ 1 14-oz. can of fat-free chicken broth
- ☐ 1 medium white onion
- ☐ 2 celery stalks
- ☐ 1 medium green bell pepper
- ☐ 1 14-oz. can of chopped tomatoes
- ☐ 1 15-oz. can of black beans
- ☐ 1 bunch of fresh cilantro

## From Your Pantry:

- ☐ garlic, ground cumin, crushed red pepper flakes, Worcestershire sauce, cooking spray

# Chicken Breasts with Tomatoes & Roasted Garlic

| | |
|---|---|
| 1 head | garlic |
| 4 | boneless, skinless chicken breasts |
| 1/2 c. | all-purpose flour |
| 1/2 t. | salt |
| 1/4 t. | ground black pepper |
| 1/2 c. | fat-free chicken broth |
| 1 medium | onion, chopped |
| 1 14-1/2 oz. | can diced tomatoes |
| 1 T. | fresh parsley, minced |
| 1 t. | ground oregano |

To roast the garlic, remove any excess papery skin. Slice off the top of the garlic head, exposing the tops of the individual garlic cloves. Spray the intact head with cooking spray and wrap it in aluminum foil. Bake in a 180°F oven for 45 minutes. Remove the garlic and squeeze out the roasted garlic meat. Set aside.

Preheat the oven to 350°F. Spray a large skillet with cooking spray and heat over medium-high heat. Dip both sides of the chicken breasts into the flour and then place them in the skillet. Cook the chicken breasts until they are golden brown. Add the salt and pepper.

Spray a 9-inch baking dish with cooking spray. Place the browned chicken breasts in the pan. Pour the chicken broth over the chicken and then layer the chopped onion and the roasted garlic. Pour the tomatoes over the onion and garlic and then sprinkle the entire pan with the fresh parsley and oregano. Bake for 35 to 40 minutes or until the chicken is completely cooked through. Makes 4 servings.

| | |
|---|---|
| Calories: | 182 |
| Total Fat: | 1g |
| Saturated Fat: | <1g |
| % Calories from Fat: | 6 |
| Carbohydrates: | 22g |
| Protein: | 20g |
| Cholesterol: | 41mg |
| Sodium: | 492mg |

Kids can help with this recipe:

1. Apply cooking spray to the topped head of garlic and wrap in aluminum foil.
2. Squeeze out the roasted garlic meat when it has cooled.
3. Wash the parsley and remove the leaves.
4. Measure the flour and dip the chicken breasts in it.
5. Measure the salt and pepper and season the chicken breasts.
6. With supervision, older kids can open the cans of chicken broth and tomatoes with a can opener.
7. Measure the chicken broth and pour over the chicken breasts. Add the chopped onion and roasted garlic.
8. Pour the tomatoes over the onion, garlic, and chicken.
9. Measure the oregano and parsley and sprinkle over the dish.

# Your Shopping List:

- ☐ 1 head garlic
- ☐ 4 boneless, skinless chicken breasts
- ☐ 1 14-oz. can of fat-free chicken broth
- ☐ 1 medium white onion
- ☐ 1 14-1/2 oz. can of diced tomatoes
- ☐ 1 bunch of fresh Italian flat-leaf parsley

## From Your Pantry:

- ☐ flour, salt, black pepper, ground oregano

## quick tip

Prepare the roasted garlic up to 2 days in advance. Remove the roasted garlic meat and store in olive oil in an airtight container. Roasted garlic is also great in mashed potatoes, mixed with olive oil to make a flavoring paste, or mixed with a mayonnaise base to form an aioli. Its sweet, nutty, mellow flavor is a welcome alternative to the sometimes astringent taste of fresh garlic.

# Honey-Mustard and Dill Chicken

| | |
|---|---|
| 1 clove | garlic, minced |
| 4 | boneless, skinless chicken breasts |
| 1/4 t. | ground black pepper |
| 1/3 c. | fat-free sour cream |
| 1/3 c. | fat-free chicken broth |
| 2 T. | Dijon mustard |
| 2 T. | honey |
| 1/4 t. | fresh dill |
| 2 T. | fat-free butter-flavored sprinkles |
| 2 slices | red onion |
| | fresh dill for garnish |

Spray a skillet with cooking spray. Heat the skillet on medium high heat and add the garlic. Stir until lightly browned and then add the chicken breasts. Brown both sides of the chicken breasts and sprinkle with the black pepper. Reduce the heat to low.

In a small bowl, combine the sour cream, chicken broth, Dijon mustard, honey, dill weed, and butter-flavored sprinkles. Pour this over the chicken breasts in the skillet and top with the onions. Increase the heat to medium, cover the skillet and simmer for 15 to 20 minutes or until the chicken is cooked through and the sauce is thickened. Garnish with fresh dill. Makes 4 servings.

| | |
|---|---|
| Calories: | 124 |
| Total Fat: | 2g |
| Saturated Fat: | <1g |
| % Calories from Fat: | 11 |
| Carbohydrates: | 9g |
| Protein: | 19g |
| Cholesterol: | 45mg |
| Sodium: | 300mg |

## quick tip

You can make the sour cream mixture in advance and refrigerate it in an airtight container overnight. The next day, when you're pressed for time, you can throw together this healthy recipe without even thinking.

Kids can help with this recipe:

1. Apply cooking spray to a skillet.

2. Mince the garlic in a garlic press.

3. Measure the black pepper and season the chicken.

4. Older kids, with supervision, can open the can of chicken broth with a can opener.

5. Measure the sour cream, chicken broth, Dijon mustard, dill weed, and butter-flavored sprinkles and combine.

6. Pour the sour cream mixture over the chicken breasts.

7. Top the chicken breasts with red onion.

# Your Shopping List:

- [ ] 4 boneless, skinless chicken breasts
- [ ] 1 8-oz. container of fat-free sour cream
- [ ] 1 14-oz. can of fat-free chicken broth
- [ ] 1 bunch of fresh dill
- [ ] 1 small red onion

## From Your Pantry:

- [ ] garlic, black pepper, Dijon mustard, honey, fat-free butter-flavored sprinkles, cooking spray

# Far East Sesame Chicken

| | |
|---|---|
| 1/2 c. | rice wine vinegar |
| 1/2 c. | low sodium soy sauce |
| 1 T. | yellow onion, chopped |
| 1/4 t. | ground ginger |
| 2 cloves | garlic, minced |
| 4 | boneless, skinless chicken breasts |
| 1/4 c. | all-purpose flour |
| 1/4 t. | ground black pepper |
| 1 T. | sesame seeds |
| 3 T. | green onions, thinly sliced |

In a medium bowl, whisk together the rice vinegar, soy sauce, onion, ground ginger, and garlic. In a sealed container, marinate the chicken breasts in this marinade for 2 to 3 hours or overnight.

Remove the chicken from the marinade and discard the marinade. Spray a large skillet with cooking spray. Heat the skillet over low heat. Lightly coat each chicken breast with flour and then place it in the skillet. Season the chicken breasts with the pepper and the sesame seeds. Sauté until the chicken is completely cooked and golden brown (about 10 minutes). Sprinkle with green onions. Makes 4 servings.

| | |
|---|---|
| Calories: | 171 |
| Total Fat: | 2g |
| Saturated Fat: | <1g |
| % Calories from Fat: | 13 |
| Carbohydrates: | 13g |
| Protein: | 21g |
| Cholesterol: | 41mg |
| Sodium: | 1064mg |

**quick tip**

There are several delicious sesame marinades on the market. You can pick up a bottle of marinade and use this to flavor the chicken.

Kids can help with this recipe:

1. Mince the garlic with a garlic press.

2. Measure the rice wine vinegar, soy sauce, onion, and ground ginger into a medium bowl. Add the minced garlic. Stir to combine.

3. Place the chicken in the marinade.

4. Apply cooking spray to a large skillet.

5. Measure the flour and coat the chicken breasts in it.

6. Measure the black pepper and sesame seeds and season the chicken.

7. Sprinkle the green onions over the finished dish.

**Teachable Moment:** This recipe provides a terrific opportunity to introduce sesame seeds to your child helper. Sesame seeds were first grown in Assyria in 3000 B.C. and have since spread throughout the world. Sesame seeds can be white, brown, black, and even red. America was first introduced to sesame seeds by African slaves.

# Your Shopping List:

- ☐ 1 small yellow onion
- ☐ 4 boneless, skinless chicken breasts
- ☐ 1 bunch of green onions

## From Your Pantry:

- ☐ rice wine vinegar, low sodium soy sauce, ground ginger, garlic, all-purpose flour, black pepper, sesame seeds

# Cajun-Spiced Chicken Breasts

| | |
|---|---|
| 4 | boneless, skinless chicken breasts |
| 1/2 t. | salt |
| 1/4 t. | ground black pepper |
| 1/2 t. | garlic powder |
| 1/2 t. | Cajun spice |
| 1 c. | bottled chili sauce |
| 1 t. | prepared horseradish |
| 3/4 c. | fat-free chicken broth |
| 1 large | yellow onion, sliced |

Preheat the oven to 350°F. Spray a large skillet with cooking spray. Brown the chicken breasts on both sides. While cooking, season the chicken with the salt, pepper, garlic powder, and Cajun spice.

Spray a 9-inch square baking pan with cooking spray. Arrange the browned chicken breasts in the pan. In a small bowl, combine the chili sauce, horseradish, and the chicken broth. Pour this over the chicken and cover with the onions. Cover the pan tightly with aluminum foil and bake for 25 minutes. Uncover and bake for another 15 to 20 minutes or until the chicken is tender and cooked through. Makes 4 servings.

| | |
|---|---|
| Calories: | 178 |
| Total Fat: | 1g |
| Saturated Fat: | <1g |
| % Calories from Fat: | 5 |
| Carbohydrates: | 24g |
| Protein: | 17g |
| Cholesterol: | 42mg |
| Sodium: | 2338mg |

## quick tip

You can prepare the chicken breast seasonings and the chili sauce mixture the night before. By doing so, you can quickly prepare this dish when you are in a rush but still want a healthy, home-cooked meal.

Kids can help with this recipe:

1. Apply cooking spray to a large skillet.
2. Measure the salt, pepper, garlic powder, and Cajun spice.
3. Older kids can, with supervision, open the can of chicken broth with a can opener.
4. Measure and combine the chili sauce, horseradish, and chicken broth. Pour over the chicken in the baking pan.
5. Cover the chicken with the onion slices.

## Your Shopping List:

- ❑ 4 boneless, skinless chicken breasts
- ❑ 1 12-oz. bottle of prepared chili sauce
- ❑ 1 14-oz. can of fat-free chicken broth
- ❑ 1 large yellow onion

## From Your Pantry:

- ❑ salt, black pepper, garlic powder, Cajun spice, prepared horseradish, cooking spray

# Salmon Cakes with Zesty Horseradish Sauce

| | |
|---|---|
| 2 T. | prepared horseradish |
| 1/2 c. | fat-free mayonnaise, divided |
| 3 t. | onion powder |
| 3 t. | fresh lemon juice |
| 3/4 t. | hot pepper sauce |
| 2 | egg whites, slightly beaten |
| 2 6 oz. | cans salmon, drained |
| 3/4 c. | seasoned breadcrumbs |
| 1/2 t. | garlic powder |
| 2 T. | fresh parsley, minced |
| 1-1/2 t. | dry mustard |
| 1/4 t. | cayenne pepper |

Combine the horseradish, 1/4 cup plus 1 tablespoon of mayonnaise, onion powder, lemon juice and hot pepper sauce in a small bowl. Mix well and cover. Refrigerate until ready to serve.

Combine the egg whites, salmon, seasoned breadcrumbs, 3 tablespoons of mayonnaise, garlic powder, parsley, dry mustard and the cayenne pepper. Mix well. Shape into 8 patties.

Spray a large skillet with cooking spray. Heat the skillet over medium-high heat and cook 4 salmon cakes for 3 to 5 minutes per side. Do not overcrowd the salmon in the skillet. When the salmon cakes are ready, remove them from the heat and cover them with foil to keep warm. Cook the remaining salmon patties. Serve the salmon cakes with the horseradish sauce. Makes 4 servings, 2 salmon cakes each.

| | |
|---|---|
| Calories: | 217 |
| Total Fat: | 5g |
| Saturated Fat: | 1g |
| % Calories from Fat: | 21 |
| Carbohydrates: | 25g |
| Protein: | 19g |
| Cholesterol: | 46mg |
| Sodium: | 1238mg |

## quick tip

Many seafood departments of grocery stores now offer freshly prepared salmon cakes. These store-bought salmon cakes will be higher in fat than the cakes from this recipe but much more convenient. You can use these cakes, but serve them with your horseradish sauce for a homemade touch.

Kids can help with this recipe:

1. Squeeze the lemons for their juice. Remove any seeds.
2. Measure the horseradish, 1/4 cup plus 1 T. mayonnaise, onion powder, lemon juice, and hot pepper sauce. Combine in a small bowl.
3. Older kids, with supervision, can open the canned salmon with a can opener.
4. Wash the parsley and remove the leaves.
5. Measure and combine the egg whites, salmon, breadcrumbs, 3 T. mayonnaise, garlic powder, parsley, dry mustard, and cayenne pepper.
6. Apply cooking spray to a large skillet.

**Teachable Moment:** It's a great time to introduce spicy, hot horseradish! Explain to your child helper that this is an ancient herb that originally came from Eastern Europe. You can buy fresh horseradish as a large white root or bottled horseradish (either white or red). It is pungent and spicy.

# Your Shopping List:

- ☐ 2 fresh lemons, for their juice
- ☐ 2 eggs or 1 8-oz. container of egg whites
- ☐ 2 6-oz. cans of salmon
- ☐ 1 bunch of fresh Italian flat-leaf parsley

# From Your Pantry:

- ☐ prepared horseradish, fat-free mayonnaise, onion powder, hot pepper sauce, seasoned bread crumbs, garlic powder, dry mustard, cayenne pepper, cooking spray

# Cowboy Stew

| | |
|---|---|
| 1 lb. | ground chicken or turkey breast |
| 1 clove | garlic, minced |
| 1 small | onion, chopped |
| 1-1/4 oz. | pkg. dry taco seasoning mix |
| 4 c. | water |
| 1 10-3/4 oz. | can cream of mushroom soup |
| 1/4 c. | celery, chopped |
| 1 1-oz. | pkg. dry ranch dressing mix |
| 5 | carrots, cut into chunks |
| 2 large | potatoes, peeled and cut into chunks |
| 1/4 t. | ground black pepper |
| 3/4 c. | fat-free sour cream |

In a large skillet sprayed with cooking spray, brown the ground meat, garlic, and onion. Add the taco seasoning and the water. Stir well. Add the mushroom soup, celery, dressing mix, and the carrots. Simmer, covered, for 15 minutes. Add the potatoes and the black pepper. Cover and simmer for 30 minutes or until the potatoes are tender and the stew is heated through. Stir in the sour cream. Serve immediately. Makes 8 servings.

| | |
|---|---|
| Calories: | 301 |
| Total Fat: | 13g |
| Saturated Fat: | 4g |
| % Calories from Fat: | 39 |
| Carbohydrates: | 26g |
| Protein: | 20g |
| Cholesterol: | 69mg |
| Sodium: | 950mg |

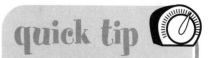

## quick tip

After browning the meat, garlic, and onion, you can place all the ingredients (except for the sour cream) in a slow cooker and cook on low for 8 hours. When you're ready to serve, stir in the sour cream. Prepared like this in advance, this hearty meal will be waiting for you and your family when you return home from a hectic day.

Kids can help with this recipe:

1. Apply cooking spray to a large skillet.

2. Mince the garlic with a garlic press.

3. Measure the water.

4. Older kids can, with supervision, open the can of mushroom soup with a can opener.

5. Wash the celery, carrots, and potatoes.

6. Peel the carrots with a child-safe vegetable peeler.

7. Measure the pepper.

8. Measure the sour cream.

**Teachable Moment:** Let your child helper know that this is called "Cowboy Stew" because it was something cowboys could cook on the campfire while out on the Western range.

# Your Shopping List:

- ❑ 1 lb. ground chicken or turkey breast
- ❑ 1 small yellow onion
- ❑ 1 1-1/4 oz. dry taco seasoning mix packet
- ❑ 1 10-3/4 oz. can of cream of mushroom soup
- ❑ 1 celery stalk
- ❑ 1 1-oz. package of dry ranch dressing mix
- ❑ 5 medium carrots
- ❑ 2 large potatoes
- ❑ 1 8-oz. container of fat-free sour cream

# From Your Pantry:

- ❑ garlic, salt, black pepper, cooking spray

# Minestrone Soup

| | |
|---|---|
| 8 c. | fat-free chicken broth |
| 1 c. | carrots, chopped |
| 1/4 c. | celery, chopped |
| 1 c. | onions, chopped |
| 1 clove | garlic, minced |
| 1-1/2 c. | canned white beans, drained |
| 1 15-oz. | can Italian-style stewed tomatoes |
| 1-1/2 t. | dried Italian seasoning |
| 1/4 t. | crushed red pepper |
| 1-1/2 c. | fresh green cabbage, shredded |
| 1 c. | fusilli, uncooked |
| 3/4 c. | low fat Parmesan cheese, grated |

Lightly spray a stockpot with cooking spray. Pour 1 tablespoon of the chicken broth into the pan and heat over medium high heat. Add the carrots, celery, onions, and garlic and simmer for 2 to 3 minutes until the vegetables are tender. Add the remaining chicken broth, white beans, stewed tomatoes, Italian seasoning, and the red pepper. Bring the soup to a boil and then reduce the heat; cover the pan and simmer for 30 to 45 minutes.

Remove the cover and add the cabbage and pasta to the soup. Bring to a boil over high heat, and then reduce the heat and simmer until the pasta is cooked al dente. Serve in individual bowls with Parmesan cheese sprinkled over each serving. Makes 6 servings.

| | |
|---|---|
| Calories: | 200 |
| Total Fat: | 3g |
| Saturated Fat: | <1g |
| % Calories from Fat: | 14 |
| Carbohydrates: | 34g |
| Protein: | 12g |
| Cholesterol: | 6mg |
| Sodium: | 726mg |

## quick tip

Minestrone soup is a fantastic way to cook extra summer vegetables. Zucchini, squash, tomatoes, corn, and green beans are all great additions to this tasty soup.

Kids can help with this recipe:

1. Wash the carrots, celery, and cabbage.
2. Peel the carrots with a child-safe vegetable peeler.
3. Mince the garlic with a garlic press.
4. Measure the carrots, celery, and onion.
5. With supervision, older kids can open the cans of chicken broth, beans and tomatoes with a can opener.
6. Measure the beans, Italian seasoning, and red pepper flakes.
7. Measure the green cabbage and fusilli.
8. Measure the Parmesan cheese and sprinkle over each bowl of soup.

# Your Shopping List:

- ☐ 5 14-oz. cans of fat-free chicken broth
- ☐ 2 medium carrots
- ☐ 1 celery stalk
- ☐ 2 medium yellow onions
- ☐ 1 15-oz. can of white beans
- ☐ 1 15-oz. can of Italian-style stewed tomatoes
- ☐ 1/2 head of fresh green cabbage
- ☐ 1 16-oz. package of fusilli
- ☐ 1 8-oz. container of grated low fat Parmesan cheese

# From Your Pantry:

- ☐ garlic, dried Italian seasoning, crushed red pepper, cooking spray

# Cool Summertime Gazpacho

| | |
|---|---|
| 1 6 oz. | can tomato paste |
| 1 | cucumber, peeled and chopped |
| 2 c. | fat-free chicken broth |
| 1 small | red onion, chopped |
| 1/4 t. | salt |
| 1/4 t. | garlic powder |
| 1/2 | green bell pepper, chopped |
| 1 stalk | celery, strings removed and chopped |
| dash | hot pepper sauce |
| 2 c. | water |
| | fresh parsley for garnish |

In a food processor, puree the tomato paste, cucumber, chicken broth, onion, salt, garlic powder, green pepper, celery, and the hot pepper sauce. Puree until the mixture is smooth. Pour the mixture into a refrigerator bowl and add the water. Stir to combine well. Chill. Serve cold with a sprig of parsley placed in the middle of each bowl. Makes 4 servings.

| | |
|---|---|
| Calories: | 65 |
| Total Fat: | <1g |
| Saturated Fat: | <1g |
| % Calories from Fat: | 2 |
| Carbohydrates: | 14g |
| Protein: | 3g |
| Cholesterol: | 3mg |
| Sodium: | 385mg |

**quick tip**

You can also add fresh tomatoes to this recipe for a chunkier texture. Fresh garlic, instead of the garlic powder, is also a welcome substitution. This Spanish-style summer soup can be made a day in advance and refrigerated to be chilled before serving.

Kids can help with this recipe:

1. Older kids can, with supervision, open the cans of tomato paste and chicken broth with a can opener.

2. Wash the cucumber and peel with a child-safe vegetable peeler.

3. Wash and deseed the green pepper.

4. Measure the chicken broth, salt, garlic powder, and hot pepper sauce. Add to the vegetables in the food processor.

5. Measure the water and add to the finished mixture. Stir to combine.

**Teachable Moment:** Let your child helper know that this is a traditional Spanish salad that has been turned into soup. This soup-salad was popularized by the Spanish wife of French Emperor Napoleon III.

# Your Shopping List:

- ❑ 1 6-oz. can of tomato paste
- ❑ 1 large cucumber
- ❑ 2 14-oz. cans of fat-free chicken broth
- ❑ 1 small red onion
- ❑ 1 medium green bell pepper
- ❑ 1 celery stalk
- ❑ 1 bunch of fresh curly-leaf parsley

## From Your Pantry:

- ❑ salt, garlic powder, hot pepper sauce

# Winter Vegetable & Barley Soup

| | |
|---|---|
| 6 c. | fat-free chicken broth |
| 1/2 c. | pearl barley |
| 2 | turnips, cut into 3/4 inch chunks |
| 1 c. | celery, diced |
| 1 c. | carrots, sliced |
| 1/2 c. | white onion, chopped |
| 1 16-oz. | can white beans, undrained |
| 1/4 t. | ground black pepper |

In a stockpot over high heat, combine the chicken broth, barley, turnips, celery, carrots, and the onions. Bring to a boil, reduce the heat to low, and simmer for 30 to 35 minutes. Add the white beans with their liquid and the black pepper. Simmer for another 10 minutes. Serve hot. Makes 6 servings.

**quick tip**

Using chicken broth in a soup gives it an all-day simmered taste even though you may have cooked it for less than an hour.

| Calories: | 190 |
|---|---|
| Total Fat: | 1g |
| Saturated Fat: | <1g |
| % Calories from Fat: | 3 |
| Carbohydrates: | 37g |
| Protein: | 10g |
| Cholesterol: | 5mg |
| Sodium: | 447mg |

Kids can help with this recipe:

1. Older kids can, with supervision, open the cans of chicken broth and white beans with a can opener.

2. Clean the vegetables and peel with a child-safe peeler, where necessary.

3. Measure the chicken broth, barley, celery, carrots, and white onion, and add to the stockpot. Also add the turnip chunks.

4. Measure the black pepper.

# Your Shopping List:

- ☐ 4 14-oz. cans of fat-free chicken broth
- ☐ 1 16-oz. bag of pearl barley
- ☐ 2 medium turnips
- ☐ 1 celery stalk
- ☐ 2 medium carrots
- ☐ 1 small white onion
- ☐ 1 16-oz. can of white beans

## From Your Pantry:
- ☐ black pepper

# Crab Pasta Salad with Lemon Dressing

| | |
|---|---|
| 2 c. | small pasta shells, cooked al dente |
| 1 c. | fresh broccoli, finely chopped |
| 1 small | carrot, grated |
| 6 oz. | cooked crab meat |
| 1 T. | white onion, finely chopped |
| 1 T. | fresh Italian flat-leaf parsley, minced |

**Lemon Dressing:**

| | |
|---|---|
| 1/2 c. | fat-free mayonnaise |
| 2 t. | lemon juice |
| 3 T. | water |
| dash | seasoned salt |
| dash | hot pepper sauce |
| dash | garlic salt |

In a small bowl, combine the mayonnaise, lemon juice, water, seasoned salt, hot pepper sauce, and the garlic salt. In a large bowl, combine the pasta, broccoli, carrot, crab meat, onion, and parsley. Gently stir to mix. Pour the salad dressing over the salad and stir gently again. Chill at least 1 hour before serving. Makes 4 servings.

| | |
|---|---|
| Calories: | 130 |
| Total Fat: | 1g |
| Saturated Fat: | <1g |
| % Calories from Fat: | 6 |
| Carbohydrates: | 23g |
| Protein: | 9g |
| Cholesterol: | 38mg |
| Sodium: | 643mg |

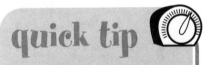

## quick tip

Some seafood departments of grocery stores offer cleaned, pre-cooked lump crabmeat. You could also use a good quality canned crabmeat. Also, check the salad dressing aisle for a low fat creamy lemon dressing to use in place of preparing one.

Kids can help with this recipe:

1. Fill a stockpot with water to cook the pasta.

2. Squeeze the lemons for their juice and remove any seeds.

3. Measure the mayonnaise, lemon juice, water, seasoned salt, hot pepper sauce, and garlic salt, and combine in a small bowl.

4. Clean the broccoli florets, carrot, and parsley. Peel the carrot with a child-safe peeler. Remove the leaves from the parsley.

5. Measure the pasta, prepared vegetables, and parsley. Add to the crab in a large bowl.

# Your Shopping List:

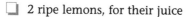

- [ ] 1 16-oz. container of small pasta shells
- [ ] 1 12-oz. bag of fresh broccoli florets (or **14** oz. frozen)
- [ ] 1 small carrot
- [ ] 6 oz. fresh crab meat
- [ ] 1 small white onion
- [ ] 1 bunch of fresh Italian flat-leaf parsley
- [ ] 2 ripe lemons, for their juice

## From Your Pantry:

- [ ] fat-free mayonnaise, seasoned salt, hot pepper sauce, garlic salt

# Tuna Niçoise Salad

| | |
|---|---|
| 1-1/2 lbs. | fresh petite green beans (or haricots vert), steamed until tender-crisp |
| 1/2 small | red onion, thinly sliced |
| 3 medium | red potatoes, cooked and sliced |
| 1-1/2 c. | cherry tomatoes |
| 18 oz. | low fat tuna, drained |
| 3/4 c. | bottled fat-free red wine vinaigrette salad dressing |
| 4 c. | spring mix lettuce leaves |
| 1/2 c. | Niçoise olives, pitted if you desire |
| 2 T. | non-pareil capers, rinsed |
| 1/4 t. | fresh ground black pepper |
| 1 T. | fresh parsley, chopped |

In a mixing bowl, combine the green beans, onion, red potatoes, cherry tomatoes, and tuna. Stir lightly to combine. Pour the salad dressing over the vegetables and tuna and toss. On a large serving platter, spread the mixed lettuce leaves. Top with the seasoned vegetables and tuna. Sprinkle the top with the olives, capers, fresh ground black pepper, and parsley. Serve immediately. Makes 6 servings.

| | |
|---|---|
| Calories: | 191 |
| Total Fat: | 5g |
| Saturated Fat: | <1g |
| % Calories from Fat: | 19 |
| Carbohydrates: | 18g |
| Protein: | 26g |
| Cholesterol: | 0mg |
| Sodium: | 985mg |

## quick tip

Although fresh is always better, you could defrost a 14 oz. bag of frozen petite green beans instead of preparing the fresh beans. Also, make sure to experiment with the wide variety of pre-washed, bagged lettuces in the produce section of your supermarket. These lettuces are easy to use and keep up to a week in your crisper. Salad making has never been easier!

Kids can help with this recipe:

1. Clean and destem the green beans to prepare for steaming.

2. Clean the red potatoes with a vegetable scrubber before cooking.

3. Wash the cherry tomatoes and measure.

4. Older kids can, with supervision, open the cans of tuna with a can opener.

5. Measure the red wine vinaigrette and pour over tuna, green beans, potatoes, and cherry tomatoes.

6. Measure the lettuce leaves and spread over a large serving platter.

7. Pit the olives, if you desire.

8. Measure the olives, capers, black pepper, and parsley. Sprinkle over the salad.

**Teachable Moment:** Olives are an ancient food that have been found in Egyptian tombs dating from 2000 B.C. Historians believe that olives have been cultivated in the Mediterranean since before written language was developed! Olives grow on trees. When freshly picked, they are bitter and their final flavor depends on the way in which they are processed or cured. They are placed in brine or packed in salt.

# Your Shopping List:

- ❑ 1-1/2 lbs. fresh petite green beans (or haricots vert)
- ❑ 1 small red onion
- ❑ 3 medium red potatoes
- ❑ 10-oz. container of cherry tomatoes
- ❑ 3 6-oz. cans of low fat tuna, drained
- ❑ 1 bottle fat-free red wine vinaigrette salad dressing
- ❑ 2 5-oz. bags of spring mix lettuce leaves
- ❑ 1 small jar of Niçoise olives
- ❑ 1 4-oz. jar of non-pareil capers
- ❑ 1 bunch of fresh Italian flat-leaf parsley

# From Your Pantry:
- ❑ black pepper

# Eggplant Parmesan

| | |
|---|---|
| 1 medium | eggplant, peeled and cut into 1/2-inch slices |
| 2 | egg whites, slightly beaten |
| 2 c. | corn flakes, crushed |
| 3/4 c. | low fat Parmesan cheese, grated |
| 1/2 c. | nonfat mozzarella cheese, shredded |
| 1 15-oz. | can stewed chopped tomatoes |
| 1 small | white onion, chopped |
| 1 t. | garlic powder |
| 1/4 t. | ground black pepper |

Preheat the oven to 350°F. Spray a 9" x 13" baking pan with cooking spray. Dip the eggplant slices in the egg whites and roll in corn flakes. Brown the eggplant slices lightly in a skillet that has been sprayed with cooking spray. Layer the browned eggplant in the prepared baking pan. Sprinkle the eggplant with the Parmesan cheese and the mozzarella cheese. Gently pour the tomatoes over the entire casserole. Sprinkle the onions over the top of the tomatoes and season with the garlic powder and black pepper. Bake, uncovered, for 45 to 50 minutes or until the eggplant is tender and cooked through. Makes 6 servings.

| | |
|---|---|
| Calories: | 140 |
| Total Fat: | 2g |
| Saturated Fat: | <1g |
| % Calories from Fat: | 13 |
| Carbohydrates: | 24g |
| Protein: | 8g |
| Cholesterol: | 3mg |
| Sodium: | 586mg |

quick tip

You can also use a prepared fat-free marinara sauce in place of the stewed tomatoes, garlic powder, and black pepper.

Kids can help with this recipe:

1. Apply cooking spray to a baking pan and large skillet.
2. Measure and crush the cornflakes.
3. Dip the eggplant slices into the egg whites and roll in the cornflakes.
4. Measure the Parmesan cheese and mozzarella cheese. Sprinkle over the browned eggplant in the baking pan.
5. Older kids, with supervision, can open the can of tomatoes with a can opener.
6. Pour the tomatoes over the casserole.
7. Sprinkle the onions on top.
8. Measure the garlic powder and black pepper. Sprinkle on top.

# Your Shopping List:

- ❏ 1 medium eggplant
- ❏ 2 eggs or 1 16-oz. container of egg whites
- ❏ 1 12-oz. box of corn flakes
- ❏ 1 5-oz. container of grated low fat Parmesan cheese
- ❏ 1 8-oz. container of shredded nonfat mozzarella cheese
- ❏ 1 15-oz. can of stewed chopped tomatoes
- ❏ 1 small white onion

## From Your Pantry:
- ❏ garlic powder, black pepper, cooking spray

# Pineapple & Banana Smoothie

| | |
|---|---|
| 1-1/2 c. | pineapple chunks, packed in juice |
| 1 small | banana, sliced |
| 3/4 c. | fat-free pineapple yogurt |
| 1/3 c. | pineapple-orange juice |
| 4 to 5 | ice cubes |

Combine the pineapple, banana, yogurt, and pineapple-orange juice in a blender or food processor. Process until smooth. Add 4 to 5 ice cubes and process until thick and creamy. Serve immediately. Makes 2 servings.

| | |
|---|---|
| Calories: | 235 |
| Total Fat: | <1g |
| Saturated Fat: | <1g |
| % Calories from Fat: | 1 |
| Carbohydrates: | 54g |
| Protein: | 5g |
| Cholesterol: | 2mg |
| Sodium: | 75mg |

## quick tip

You can also use 2 tablespoons of frozen pineapple-orange juice concentrate instead of the prepared juice. Just add 1/3 cup of water, milk, or soymilk. Instead of ice cubes, you can also use an equal amount of pineapple sherbet for even richer flavor and texture.

Kids can help with this recipe:

1. Older kids can, with supervision, open the can of pineapple with a can opener.
2. Measure the pineapple chunks.
3. Peel and slice the banana with a butter knife.
4. Measure the yogurt and juice.
5. Place all ingredients in a blender or food processor.

**Teachable Moment:** If using fresh pineapple, let your child-helper examine the outside of the pineapple, carefully touching the rough skin and spiny leaves. It is called a pineapple because when Europeans first saw it, they thought it looked like a pinecone with the flesh of an apple. Each pineapple takes 18 months to grow and is cultivated in warm, tropical areas such as Hawaii and Central America.

# Your Shopping List:

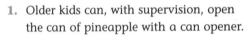

- ☐ 1 20-oz. can of pineapple chunks, packed in juice
- ☐ 1 small banana
- ☐ 1 6-oz. container of fat-free pineapple yogurt
- ☐ 1 small carton of pineapple-orange juice

# It Only Takes A
# Sweet Moment

The perfect way to end a delicious meal is with a touch of sweetness. This chapter provides you with foolproof recipes for quick and easy dessert ideas that everyone will enjoy. Many of these recipes can be made in advance so that you can enjoy dinner without worrying about actually preparing a complicated dessert to end the evening. Additionally, these recipes utilize ingredients from your fully-stocked pantry so that you only have to buy a few needed ingredients during your trip to the grocery store. Most importantly, all of the featured desserts are so sinfully luxurious and decadent that your family and guests will never guess how simple they were to make!

By the end of this chapter, you will:

- prepare tasty, mouth-watering desserts in a time-efficient manner
- know how to utilize store-bought ingredients as shortcuts
- learn which flavor combinations are the best for desserts
- employ your child helpers in the kitchen and teach them basic baking skills
- excite your child helpers with fun facts about dessert ingredients
- make your grocery shopping even speedier with our comprehensive lists
- use your pantry as an amazing resource for making dessert
- surprise your family with luscious endings to their dinner meals
- feel confident that you can create incredible desserts with limited effort and time

# Lunchbox Walnut Oatmeal Cookies

| | |
|---|---|
| 18-1/4 oz. | yellow cake mix |
| 2 c. | quick-cooking oats |
| 1 c. | sugar |
| 1 c. | vegetable oil |
| 2 | eggs |
| 1 c. | walnuts, chopped |
| 1 t. | vanilla extract |

Preheat the oven to 350ºF. Combine the cake mix, oats, and sugar in a large bowl. Add the oil and eggs and beat well to blend. Add the walnuts and vanilla and beat again. Drop the dough by rounded teaspoons on a lightly greased baking sheet. Bake for 10 minutes. Do not overbake. Makes about 2-1/2 dozen cookies.

Kids can help with this recipe:

1. Measure the oats and sugar. Combine with the cake mix in a large bowl.

2. Measure the oil and add to the oat mixture. Add the eggs. Blend well.

3. Measure the walnuts and vanilla and add to the mixture. Beat well.

4. Drop the cookie dough by rounded teaspoons on the baking sheet.

**Teachable Moment:** This is a wonderful occasion to teach your child helper about walnuts. Let them examine an unshelled walnut and have them feel the bumpy texture of the shell. Explain that the shell protects the inside meat. Tell them that humans started roasting walnuts over fires more than 8,000 years ago.

# Your Shopping List:

- ❑ 1 18-1/4 oz. package of yellow cake mix
- ❑ 2 eggs
- ❑ 7 oz. bag of shelled walnuts

## From Your Pantry:

- ❑ quick-cooking oats, sugar, vegetable oil, vanilla extract

# quick tip

Check out the selection of nuts in your local supermarket. To save time, select shelled, pre-chopped nuts whenever a recipe calls for chopped nuts of any kind. Just make sure that they are unsalted.

# Quick Almond & Coconut Squares

| | |
|---|---|
| 1/2 c. | butter, melted |
| 1 c. | brown sugar |
| 1 c. | quick-cooking oats |
| 1 c. | flaked coconut |
| 1/2 c. | almonds, sliced |
| 6 oz. | semi-sweet chocolate chips |
| 1 t. | vanilla |

Preheat the oven to 350ºF. Mix together in a large bowl all of the ingredients. Spoon the dough into a greased 8" x 8" baking pan, and use a knife to create a smooth and even top. Bake for 20 to 25 minutes. Cool for 10 minutes and cut into 16 squares. Remove when cooled completely. Makes 16 squares.

Kids can help with this recipe:

1. Measure all of the ingredients and mix together in a large bowl.
2. Spoon the dough into a baking pan.

**Teachable Moment:** Coconuts are the fruit of the coconut palm, which is originally from Malaysia. Each coconut palm produces thousands of coconuts over the course of its lifetime. Each coconut has several layers with an interior layer of creamy coconut meat and coconut juice. If you have a chance, let your child helper examine a real coconut from the store, and explain that the coconut meat, coconut milk, and coconut cream can all be bought separately.

# Your Shopping List:

- ❏ 1 14-oz. bag of flaked coconut
- ❏ 1 5-oz. bag of sliced almonds
- ❏ 1 11-oz. bag of semi-sweet chocolate chips

## From Your Pantry:

- ❏ butter, brown sugar, quick-cooking oats, vanilla

## quick tip

Although these bars are fantastic on their own, they can also be the foundation of an elegantly decadent but simple dessert worthy of special occasions. Place a warm bar in the bottom of a dessert bowl. Top with a scoop of vanilla bean ice cream. Drizzle warmed caramel on top and sprinkle with toasted almonds and shredded coconut. How dreamy is that?

# Decadent Chocolate Kahlua Pie

| | |
|---|---|
| 1 qt. | coffee-flavored ice cream |
| 3 T. | Kahlua® liquor |
| 1 | 9-inch prepared chocolate crumb pie shell |
| 1 c. | chocolate fudge sauce |

Soften the ice cream just until it can be mixed with the Kahlua. Blend together and spoon into the prepared pie shell. Drizzle with the fudge sauce and freeze for 15 to 20 minutes. Makes 8 servings.

Kids can help with this recipe:

1. Spoon the ice cream mixture into the prepared pie shell.
2. Measure the chocolate fudge sauce and drizzle over the ice cream.

**Teachable Moment:** This is a perfect opportunity to talk to your child about the origins of chocolate. Explain that chocolate comes from the cacao plant, which is native to Central America. The Mayans were famous chocolate makers; they would use the beans of the cacao plant to make a type of chocolate drink. The Spanish conquistadors introduced Europe to chocolate. Different types of chocolate are formed depending on the amount of cocoa butter, sugar, vanilla, and milk that is added to the processed chocolate paste called "chocolate liquor."

# Your Shopping List:

- ☐ 1 qt. coffee-flavored ice cream
- ☐ 1 9-inch prepared chocolate crumb pie shell
- ☐ 1 16-oz. jar of prepared chocolate fudge sauce

## From Your Pantry:
- ☐ Kahlua® liquor

## quick tip

Make sure to pick up the best quality coffee-flavored ice cream; it makes a huge difference in the flavor outcome of this dessert. If your ice cream is too hard, defrost it in the microwave, checking at the end of 5-second intervals until just softened.

# Orange Chocolate Muffins

| | |
|---|---|
| 1 c. | whole-wheat flour |
| 1 c. | all-purpose flour |
| 1/2 t. | salt |
| 3/4 t. | baking soda |
| 1/2 c. | sugar |
| 3 T. | unsweetened cocoa |
| 2/3 c. | buttermilk |
| 1/3 c. | orange juice |
| 1 | egg |
| 1 t. | vanilla extract |
| 2 T. | orange zest, grated |

## quick tip

A simple shortcut for this recipe is to use boxed chocolate muffin mix. Add orange juice in the place of some of its liquid ingredients as well as orange zest. Follow the package's baking instructions.

Preheat the oven to 375°F. Grease 12 medium-size muffin cups. In a large bowl, combine the flours, salt, baking soda, sugar, and the cocoa thoroughly. In a small bowl, beat together the buttermilk, orange juice, egg, and vanilla extract. Stir the zest into the buttermilk mixture. Add the buttermilk mixture to the flour mixture and stir just until the dry ingredients are moistened. Fill the muffin cups two-thirds full with batter. Bake for 18 minutes or until a toothpick inserted in the center comes out clean. Remove the muffins from the oven, cool on a wire rack for 5 minutes, and then remove the muffins from the tins to cool completely. Serve warm. Makes 12 servings.

Kids can help with this recipe:

1. Grease muffin cups.
2. Measure the flours, salt, baking soda, and cocoa. Combine in a large bowl.
3. Measure the buttermilk, orange juice, egg, and vanilla extract. Beat together in a small bowl.
4. Zest an orange. Measure the zest and add to the buttermilk mixture.
5. Add the buttermilk mixture to the flour mixture and stir.

# Your Shopping List:

- ☐ 1 2-lb. package of whole-wheat flour
- ☐ 1 pint buttermilk
- ☐ 1 half-pint orange juice
- ☐ 1 egg
- ☐ 1 orange, for its zest

## From Your Pantry:

- ☐ all-purpose flour, salt, baking soda, sugar, unsweetened cocoa, vanilla extract

# Cinnamon Hazelnut Cake
# with Whipped Cream Topping

**Cake:**

| | |
|---|---|
| 3/4 c. | butter, softened |
| 1-1/2 c. | light brown sugar, firmly packed |
| 3 | large eggs |
| 2 c. | all-purpose flour |
| 1 c. | ground hazelnuts |
| 1 t. | baking powder |
| 1 t. | baking soda |
| 1 t. | ground cinnamon |
| 1 c. | buttermilk |

**Whipped Cream Topping:**

| | |
|---|---|
| 2-1/2 c. | heavy cream, ice cold |
| 1/3 c. | sugar |
| 2 t. | vanilla extract |

Preheat the oven to 350°F. Butter and line with waxed paper a 9" x 13" baking pan. In a large mixing bowl, beat the butter and sugar together for 5 minutes until they are light and fluffy. Beat in the eggs one at a time. In a small bowl combine the flour, hazelnuts, baking powder, baking soda, and the cinnamon. Add the flour mixture to the creamed mixture alternately with the buttermilk, combining well after each addition. Pour the batter into the prepared pan. Bake for 25 to 30 minutes until a toothpick inserted in the center of the cake comes out clean.

Cool the cake in the pan on a rack for 5 minutes. Unmold the cake onto the wire rack and remove the waxed paper. Cool the cake completely.

Using a large mixing bowl, combine the heavy cream, sugar, and vanilla with an electric mixer on medium speed until it is thick and smooth (about 2 minutes).

To serve, place a piece of cake on a plate and top with a dollop of the whipped topping. Makes 12 servings.

Kids can help with this recipe:

1. Butter the baking pan.
2. Measure the butter and sugar.
3. Add the eggs as the mixture is beaten.
4. Measure the flour, hazelnuts, baking powder, baking soda, and cinnamon, and combine in a small bowl.
5. Measure the buttermilk.
6. Pour the batter into a prepared pan.
7. Measure the heavy cream, sugar, and vanilla for the topping.
8. Place a dollop of whipped topping on each serving.

## quick tip

You can also use non-dairy whipped topping or pressurized whipped cream in place of the homemade whipped topping. Garnish with chopped, toasted hazelnuts and a sprinkling of cinnamon.

# Your Shopping List:

- ❑ 3 large eggs
- ❑ 1 small package of ground hazelnuts
- ❑ 1 half-pint buttermilk
- ❑ 1-1/2 pints heavy cream

## From Your Pantry:

- ❑ butter, light brown sugar, all-purpose flour, baking powder, baking soda, ground cinnamon, sugar, vanilla extract

# Purely Spritz Cookies

| | |
|---|---|
| 2/3 c. | sugar |
| 1 c. | butter, softened |
| 1 | egg |
| 1/2 t. | salt |
| 3 t. | vanilla extract |
| 2-1/4 c. | all-purpose flour |

Preheat the oven to 400°F. In a large mixing bowl, beat the sugar, butter, egg, salt, and vanilla on medium speed until creamy. Reduce the speed to low, add the flour, and beat until well mixed. Spoon the dough into a cookie press. Form the shapes 1-inch apart on cookie sheets. Bake for 6 to 8 minutes or until the edges of the cookies are lightly browned. Remove the baked cookies to wire racks to cool. Store in an airtight container. Makes 5 dozen cookies.

Kids can help with this recipe:

1. Measure the sugar, egg, salt, and vanilla. Place in a large mixing bowl.
2. Crack the egg into the mixing bowl with the sugar.
3. Measure the flour.
4. Spoon the dough into a cookie press.

# Your Shopping List:

☐  1 egg

## From Your Pantry:
☐  sugar, butter, salt, vanilla extract, all-purpose flour

## quick tip

This is the ultimate pantry cookie. All of the ingredients listed, except the egg, should be in your pantry already. And the egg is probably in your refrigerator! This is the perfect cookie for those times when you've forgotten that the dessert potluck at work is tomorrow and the store is already closed.

# Classic Coffee Cake

**Cake:**

| | |
|---|---|
| 1/2 c. | sugar |
| 2 T. | butter, melted |
| 1 | egg |
| 1 c. | milk |
| 1-1/4 c. | all-purpose flour |
| 2 t. | baking powder |
| 1/4 t. | salt |

**Topping:**

| | |
|---|---|
| 2 T. | sugar |
| 2 t. | cinnamon |
| 1/4 c. | nuts, chopped |

Preheat the oven to 425°F. Grease a 9-inch cake pan. In a large mixing bowl, cream the sugar and the butter. In a small bowl, mix together the egg and the milk. Stir the milk mixture into the creamed butter. In a medium bowl, mix together the flour, baking powder, and salt. Stir the flour mixture into the creamed mixture just until the flour is moistened. Do not over mix. Spoon the batter into the greased pan. In a small bowl, mix together the sugar, cinnamon, and nuts. Sprinkle the crumb mixture over the cake batter. Bake for 20 to 25 minutes until the cake is nicely brown. Remove the pan from the oven and place on a wire rack to cool slightly. Cut and serve while the coffee cake is warm. Makes 6 servings.

Kids can help with this recipe:

1. Grease the cake pan.

2. Measure the sugar and butter for the batter and place in a large mixing bowl to be creamed.

3. Measure the milk. Crack the egg and combine with the milk in a small bowl.

4. Measure the flour, baking powder, and salt and combine in a medium bowl.

5. Measure the sugar, cinnamon, and nuts for the topping. Combine in a small bowl.

6. Sprinkle the cinnamon mixture over the cake batter.

**quick tip**

To make individual coffee cakes, spoon the cake batter into greased muffin tins. Top with the cinnamon mixture. Your guests will enjoy their own mini-cakes.

**Teachable Moment:** Explain to your child helper that coffee cake is a sweet, cake-like bread that is called "coffee cake" because it is usually eaten while drinking coffee. Coffee cake has many forms; it can have fruit, nuts, or even cream cheese fillings.

# Your Shopping List:

❑ 1 egg
❑ 1 8-oz. bag of nuts, your choice

## From Your Pantry:

❑ sugar, butter, milk, all-purpose flour, baking powder, salt, cinnamon

# Southern Pecan Pie

| | |
|---|---|
| 2 T. | butter, melted |
| 1 c. | light brown sugar, firmly packed |
| 2 T. | all-purpose flour |
| 2 | eggs |
| 2 t. | vanilla extract |
| 1/4 t. | salt |
| 1 c. | light corn syrup |
| 1 | 9-inch unbaked pie shell |
| 3/4 c. | pecan halves |

Preheat the oven to 375°F. In a mixing bowl, combine the butter, brown sugar, and flour thoroughly. Add the eggs, vanilla, and salt and beat again. Add the corn syrup to the batter and beat lightly. Pour the filling into the pie shell and sprinkle the pecans over the top. Bake for 35 minutes. Remove the pie from the oven and cool on a wire rack. Serve warm or cooled. Makes 8 servings.

Kids can help with this recipe:

1.  Measure the butter and place in the microwave to be melted.

2.  Measure the brown sugar and flour. Combine with the melted butter.

3.  Measure the vanilla and salt. Add to the flour mixture.

4.  Crack open 2 eggs and add them to the flour mixture.

5.  Measure the corn syrup and add.

6.  Measure the pecans and sprinkle on top of the pie.

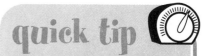

**quick tip**

If you have other nuts instead of pecans, you can use them as the topping for this deliciously easy pie. Just make sure they are unsalted.

**Teachable Moment:** The pecan nut was native to Texas and Northern Mexico and then spread to the area of Louisiana. While in Louisiana, the French were introduced to the pecan nut and settlers of New Orleans were soon making pecan pie! It was also used as a food source by Native Americans. The pecan has one of the highest fat contents of the nut family.

# Your Shopping List:

- ☐ 2 eggs
- ☐ 1 9-inch unbaked pie shell
- ☐ 1 10-oz. bag of pecan halves

## From Your Pantry:

- ☐ butter, light brown sugar, all-purpose flour, vanilla extract, salt, light corn syrup

# Layered Butterscotch Squares

| | |
|---|---|
| 1/2 c. | butter, melted |
| 1-1/2 c. | graham cracker crumbs |
| 1 3-1/2 oz. | pkg. flaked coconut |
| 1 6-oz. | pkg. butterscotch chips |
| 1 c. | chopped walnuts |
| 1 4-oz. | can sweetened condensed milk |

Preheat the oven to 375°F. Place the melted butter into the bottom of a 9" x 13" baking pan. Layer each ingredient as it is listed. Layer the graham cracker crumbs first, then the coconut, the butterscotch chips, the chopped walnuts, and then pour the condensed milk over all. Do not stir. Bake for 25 minutes. Remove the pan from the oven, cool on a wire rack and then cut into small squares. Makes 40 squares.

Kids can help with this recipe:

1.  Measure the butter and place in the microwave to be melted.
2.  Crush and measure the graham crackers.
3.  Layer the graham cracker crumbs over the melted butter.
4.  Layer the coconut over the graham cracker crumbs.
5.  Layer the butterscotch chips over the coconut.
6.  Layer the chopped walnuts over the butterscotch chips.
7.  Older kids can, with supervision, open the can of milk with a can opener.
8.  Pour the milk over the chopped walnuts.

**Teachable Moment:** What is the difference between butterscotch and caramel? Butterscotch is a blend of butter and brown sugar cooked at 270 degrees whereas caramel is sugar that is cooked until it melts and is caramelized at about 320 degrees.

# Your Shopping List:

- ☐ 1 14-1/4 oz. box of graham crackers
- ☐ 1 3-1/2 oz. package of flaked coconut
- ☐ 1 6-oz. package of butterscotch chips
- ☐ 1 10-oz. bag of chopped walnuts
- ☐ 1 4-oz. can of sweetened condensed milk

## From Your Pantry:

- ☐ butter

Use these luscious butterscotch squares as the base for a sinful dessert: raspberry butterscotch sundaes. Just top a butterscotch square with a scoop of high-quality vanilla bean ice cream, a sprinkling of fresh raspberries, and a spoonful of butterscotch sauce. Top with toasted coconut for crunch. Yum!

# Soft Gingerbread

**Gingerbread:**

| | |
|---|---|
| 2 t. | baking soda |
| 1 c. | boiling water |
| 1 c. | butter, softened |
| 3/4 c. | sugar |
| 1 c. | molasses |
| 1 t. | salt |
| 1 t. | ground ginger |
| 1 t. | ground cinnamon |
| 2-3/4 c. | all-purpose flour |
| 2 | eggs |

**Glaze:**

| | |
|---|---|
| 1/2 c. | powdered sugar |
| 1/4 c. | milk |

Preheat the oven to 350°F. Grease a 9" x 13" baking pan. In a small bowl, dissolve the baking soda in boiling water. In a large mixing bowl, cream together the butter and the sugar. Add the baking soda/water mixture, molasses, salt, ginger, cinnamon, and flour to the large mixing bowl. Mix thoroughly. Add the eggs and beat well. Pour the batter into the baking pan. Bake for 45 minutes or until a toothpick inserted in the center of the cake comes out clean. Remove the pan from the oven and place it on a wire rack to cool. Make the glaze by combining the powdered sugar and the milk. The glaze should be thin. Evenly pour the glaze over the warm ginger bread. Cut into squares and serve warm or cooled. Makes 24 squares.

**quick tip**

For added oomph, you can add minced pieces of crystallized ginger to the batter. This will give the squares more sweet spiciness and texture.

Kids can help with this recipe:

1. Grease the baking pan.

2. Measure the baking soda.

3. Measure the butter and sugar and place them in a large mixing bowl.

4. Measure the molasses, salt, ginger, cinnamon, and flour. Add to the large mixing bowl.

5. Crack open the eggs and add to the mixture.

6. Measure the powdered sugar and milk. Combine in a small bowl.

# Your Shopping List:

❑  2 eggs

## From Your Pantry:

❑  baking soda, butter, sugar, molasses, salt, ground ginger, ground cinnamon, all-purpose flour, powdered sugar, milk

# Sugar Cookies In-A-Hurry

| | |
|---|---|
| 1 c. | sugar |
| 1 c. | powdered sugar |
| 1 c. | butter |
| 2 | eggs |
| 1 c. | vegetable oil |
| 1 t. | vanilla extract |
| 1 t. | salt |
| 1 t. | baking soda |
| 1 t | cream of tartar |
| 4 c. + 2 T. | all-purpose flour |
| | sugar for dusting |

Preheat the oven to 350°F. In a large bowl, cream together the sugars and the butter. Add the eggs, oil, and vanilla. Beat well. Sift together the salt, baking soda, cream of tartar, and flour. Add the flour mixture to the creamed mixture and blend well. Drop by teaspoonfuls onto ungreased cookie sheets. Press a glass, dipped in sugar, onto the top of each cookie. Bake for 8 to 10 minutes until lightly browned. Cool the cookies on wire racks. Makes about 4 dozen.

Kids can help with this recipe:

1. Measure the sugar, powdered sugar, and butter. Place in a large bowl.
2. Crack open the eggs and add to the creamed sugar and butter.
3. Measure the oil and vanilla and add to the creamed mixture.
4. Measure the salt, baking soda, cream of tartar, and flour. Sift together and add to the creamed mixture.
5. Drop cookie dough by teaspoonfuls onto ungreased cookie sheets.
6. Press a glass, dipped in sugar, onto the top of each cookie.

**Teachable Moment:** This is a fantastic opportunity to teach your child helper about sugar. Sugar was cultivated in Persia and Arabia in 4th century B.C. but didn't make it to the Western world until 400 years later. Sugar comes in forms. White granulated sugar comes from sugarcanes or beets. Brown sugar is a combination of white sugar and molasses. Powdered or Confectioner's sugar is regular white sugar that has been crushed to a superfine, powdery consistency and mixed with a small amount of cornstarch.

# Your Shopping List:

❏  2 eggs

## From Your Pantry:

❏  sugar, powdered sugar, butter, vegetable oil, vanilla extract, salt, baking soda, cream of tartar, all-purpose flour

## quick tip

Some supermarkets carry pre-made sugar cookie dough in refrigerated or freezer sections. This can come in handy when you still want that "baked-in-the-oven cookie smell" permeating your house but simply don't have the time for all the preparation. You can dust the cookies in sugar or colorful cookie sprinkles.

# Spiced Apple & Pecan Cake

| | |
|---|---|
| 1/2 c. | butter, softened |
| 1 c. | sugar |
| 1 | egg, lightly beaten |
| 1 c. | all-purpose flour |
| 1 t. | baking soda |
| 1 t. | ground cinnamon |
| 1/2 t. | ground nutmeg |
| 1/2 t. | ground allspice |
| 1/2 t. | salt |
| 2 large | green apples, peeled, cored, and sliced |
| 1/2 c. | pecans, lightly chopped |

Preheat the oven to 350°F. Butter a 9-inch cake pan. In a large bowl, cream together the butter and the sugar until light and fluffy. Add the egg and beat well. In a separate bowl, combine the flour, soda, cinnamon, nutmeg, allspice, and salt. Add gently to the moist ingredients. Do not over mix. Stir in the apple slices and the pecans. Pour the batter into the prepared pan and bake for 30 minutes or until a toothpick inserted in the center comes out clean. Remove from the oven and place on a wire rack to cool. Makes 6 to 8 servings.

Kids can help with this recipe:

1. Butter the cake pan.
2. Measure the butter and sugar and place in the same large bowl to be creamed.
3. Crack open the egg and add to the creamed mixture.
4. Measure the flour, soda, cinnamon, nutmeg, allspice, and salt. Combine in a bowl.
5. Peel the apples with a child-safe vegetable peeler.
6. Add the sliced apples and pecans to the batter.

# quick tip

A great substitution for the apples would be pears. Pears also go well with cinnamon and nutmeg flavors and nuts. You could also use walnuts or hazelnuts for a different twist. Serve this dish warm with vanilla ice cream.

# Your Shopping List:

- ☐ 1 egg
- ☐ 2 large green cooking apples
- ☐ 1 5-oz. bag of pecans

### From Your Pantry:

☐ butter, sugar, all-purpose flour, baking soda, ground cinnamon, ground nutmeg, ground all-spice, salt

# Double Chocolate After-School Cookies

| | |
|---|---|
| 1 c. | butter, softened |
| 1-1/4 c. | sugar |
| 2 | eggs |
| 2 t. | vanilla extract |
| 2 c. | all-purpose flour |
| 2/3 c. | baking cocoa |
| 3/4 t. | baking soda |
| 1/4 t. | salt |
| 2 c. | semi-sweet chocolate chips |

Preheat the oven to 350°F. In large mixing bowl, beat together the butter, sugar, eggs, and vanilla until light and fluffy. In a separate bowl, stir together the flour, cocoa, baking soda, and salt. Add the flour mixture to the creamed mixture and mix well. Stir in the chocolate chips. Drop by rounded teaspoonfuls onto an ungreased cookie sheet. Bake for 8 to 10 minutes. Let the cookies cool on the cookie sheet, and then place them on a wire rack to finish cooling. Store in an airtight container. Makes about 4-1/2 dozen cookies.

Kids can help with this recipe:

1. Measure the butter, sugar, and vanilla. Crack open the eggs and put together in a large mixing bowl, ready to be beaten together.

2. Measure the flour, cocoa, baking soda, and salt. Sift together into a separate bowl.

3. Measure the chocolate chips and add to the batter.

4. Drop by rounded teaspoonfuls onto an ungreased cookie sheet.

# Your Shopping List:

- ☐ 2 eggs
- ☐ 1 11-oz. bag of semi-sweet chocolate chips

## From Your Pantry:

- ☐ butter, sugar, vanilla extract, all-purpose flour, baking cocoa, baking soda, salt

## quick tip

These cookies can be stored for up to 2 weeks in an airtight container. You can also freeze them for up to 2 months. Another great idea is to freeze the unbaked cookie dough in a freezer bag, baking cookies as you need them.

# Blackberry Cobbler

**Fruit:**

| | |
|---|---|
| 4 c. | blackberries, rinsed and drained |
| 2 T. | cornstarch |
| 2 T. | water |
| 3/4 t. | ground cinnamon |
| 1 t. | sugar |

**Cobbler:**

| | |
|---|---|
| 1 c. | all-purpose flour |
| 1-1/2 t. | baking powder |
| 1/2 t. | salt |
| 2 T. | margarine, melted |
| 2 T. | apple juice concentrate |
| 1/4 c. | low-fat blackberry yogurt |

Preheat the oven to 375°F. Mix the cornstarch with the water. Place the blackberries in a large bowl. Sprinkle the cinnamon and the sugar over the berries. Pour the cornstarch liquid over all and stir to mix. Pour the berries into a 9" square baking pan.

In a medium bowl, combine the flour, baking powder, and salt. Mix together the melted margarine, apple juice concentrate, and yogurt. Add the mixture to the dry ingredients just until they are moistened. Place the dough on a lightly floured surface and knead for 20 to 30 seconds. Press the dough out into a 9-inch square that will fit the pan. Lay the dough over the berries. Bake for 20 to 25 minutes until the cobbler is golden brown. Remove from the oven and serve warm. Makes 9 servings.

Kids can help with this recipe:

1. Measure the cornstarch and water. Mix them together.

2. Clean the blackberries. Measure them and place in a large bowl.

3. Measure the cinnamon and sugar and sprinkle over the berries.

4. Pour the cornstarch mixture over the berries.

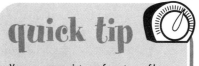

**quick tip**

You can use a mixture of any type of berry you choose. If fresh berries are unavailable, defrosted frozen berries can be used too.

5. Measure the flour, baking powder, and salt. Combine in a medium bowl.

6. Measure the margarine, apple juice concentrate, and yogurt. Add to the dry ingredients.

**Teachable Moment:** Let your child helper carefully handle a blackberry. Explain that they grow on thorny bushes called brambles and start off light green, change to red, and eventually turn a deep purple-black. They are native to the United States.

# Your Shopping List:

- ☐ 4 c. blackberries
- ☐ 1 12-oz. container of frozen apple juice concentrate
- ☐ 1 6-oz. container of low fat blackberry yogurt

## From Your Pantry:
- ☐ cornstarch, ground cinnamon, sugar, all-purpose flour, baking powder, salt, margarine

# Fudge Brownies

| | |
|---|---|
| 1 c. | butter |
| 4 oz. | unsweetened chocolate, chopped |
| 2 c. | sugar |
| 4 | eggs |
| 2 t. | vanilla extract |
| 1-1/2 c. | all-purpose flour |
| 2/3 c. | walnuts, chopped (optional) |

Preheat the oven to 325°F. Spray a 9" x 12" baking pan with cooking spray. In a medium saucepan over low heat, melt the butter and the chocolate, stirring until smooth. Remove from the heat and add the sugar. Stir until the sugar has completely dissolved. Add the eggs one at a time, mixing well after each addition. Add in the vanilla and stir. Add the flour and mix thoroughly. Stir in the chopped walnuts. Spread the batter into the prepared pan and bake for 25 minutes. Watch closely to prevent overbaking. Remove the brownies from the oven and cool on a wire rack. After the brownies have cooled for 30 minutes, cut into squares. Makes 28 large brownies.

Kids can help with this recipe:

1. Apply cooking spray to the baking pan.
2. Measure the butter and combine with the chocolate in an unheated medium saucepan.
3. Measure the sugar.
4. Measure the vanilla.
5. Measure the flour and chopped walnuts.

## Your Shopping List:

- ❏ 4 oz. unsweetened chocolate
- ❏ 4 eggs
- ❏ 1 10-oz. bag of walnuts

## From Your Pantry:

- ❏ butter, sugar, vanilla extract, all-purpose flour, cooking spray

## quick tip

For variety, try adding mini-marshmallows to the batter to create rocky road fudge brownies. Or you can add chocolate chips for extra chocolaty decadence.

# It Only Takes A Drizzle

Sometimes it only takes an elegant, sophisticated sauce to transform your entrée from boringly bland to incredibly interesting. This chapter provides you with a host of wonderful sauces and marinades to elevate your meal to that next level. Rather than using the typical seasoning for meat, poultry, or seafood, you can mix it up with some of our delicious accompaniments. Amazingly, these sauces are so simple and convenient that mostly pantry ingredients are used. Simply throw these basic ingredients together and you will create flavorings that add exceptional zing to your entrées. Even better, you can make all of these sauces in advance for added ease and flavor.

By the end of this chapter, you will:

- craft extraordinary sauces, marinades, and salsas with ordinary, simple ingredients
- learn which sauces complement chicken, turkey, pork, fish, beef, and shellfish
- enhance your meat, poultry, and seafood entrées with incomparable flavor accompaniments
- further educate your child helpers about food ingredients
- teach your child helpers cooking and measuring skills
- understand the importance of a well-stocked pantry
- streamline your grocery shopping with our useful lists
- know a fantastic library of sauces, marinades, and salsas that you can create at the drop of a hat

# Ginger & Hot Pepper Sauce

| | |
|---|---|
| 1/2 c. | dry white wine |
| 1/2 c. | soy sauce |
| 2 T. | honey |
| 2 T. | rice wine vinegar |
| 4 cloves | garlic, minced |
| 2 T. | fresh ginger, minced |
| 1/8 t. | crushed hot pepper flakes |
| 1 T. | cornstarch |
| 3 T. | cold water |

In a small saucepan, combine the wine, soy sauce, honey, rice wine vinegar, garlic, ginger, and hot pepper flakes, stirring to blend. Over medium-high heat, bring these to a boil. Reduce the heat to medium low and simmer, uncovered, for 10 minutes. In a small bowl, mix together the cornstarch and the water. When the sauce is done simmering, add the cornstarch mixture and cook, stirring, for 1 minute until the sauce is thickened. Refrigerate for up to a week. Makes about 1-1/4 cups.

Kids can help with this recipe:

1. Mince the garlic with a garlic press.

2. Grate the ginger after it has been peeled.

3. Measure the wine, soy sauce, honey, rice wine vinegar, garlic, ginger, and hot pepper flakes. Put in a small, unheated saucepan and stir to blend.

4. Measure the cornstarch and water. Mix together until smooth.

**Teachable Moment:** Rice wine vinegar is a smooth, subtle vinegar that is made from rice and Japanese sake. It is sweet but slightly tangy, and its delicate flavor is good as a seasoning for many Asian dishes.

**quick tip**

This Asian-inspired sauce gains a lot of flavor from fresh ginger. An easy way to store fresh ginger is to tightly wrap pieces in plastic wrap and place in the freezer. It will last for up to 3 months. A simple way to peel the ginger skin off of the root is to use a spoon instead of a knife.

# Your Shopping List:

❏ 2-inch stalk of fresh ginger

## From Your Pantry:

❏ dry white wine, soy sauce, honey,
rice wine vinegar, garlic, crushed hot pepper flakes, cornstarch

# Smoky Sweet Rib Sauce

| | |
|---|---|
| 1 T. | vegetable oil |
| 4 cloves | garlic, minced |
| 3-1/2 c. | crushed tomatoes in puree |
| 1/4 c. | brown sugar, firmly packed |
| 1/4 c. | molasses |
| 1/2 c. | beef broth |
| 1/4 c. | cider vinegar |
| 2 T. | Worcestershire sauce |
| 2 T. | chipoltes in adobo sauce |
| 1/2 t. | ground cloves |
| 1 t. | ground cinnamon |

In a large saucepan over medium heat, lightly brown the minced garlic in the heated oil. Add the tomatoes, brown sugar, molasses, broth, vinegar, and Worcestershire sauce, whisking to blend well. Add the chipoltes, cloves, and cinnamon. Whisk to combine. Bring the sauce to a boil and reduce the heat to low. Simmer, uncovered, until the sauce is thickened (about 30 minutes). The sauce can be refrigerated for up to a month. Makes about 4 cups.

## quick tip

Although this is a rib sauce, it can also be used for other cuts of meat as well as poultry. Because of the amount of sugar in the sauce, it's best to baste your choice of meat in the last 30 minutes of cooking to keep it from burning. You will get a spicy, sweet glaze with a subtle, smoky flavor.

Kids can help with this recipe:

1. Mince the garlic with a garlic press.
2. Measure the oil and place in a large saucepan.
3. Older kids can, with supervision, open the cans of tomatoes, beef broth, and chipotles with a can opener.
4. Measure the tomatoes, brown sugar, molasses, broth, vinegar, and Worcestershire sauce.
5. Measure the cloves and cinnamon.

**Teachable Moment:** Chipotle peppers are actually smoked, dried jalapeño peppers, with a moderately spicy taste. They are normally packed in an adobo sauce, which is a mixture of spices, tomato sauce, vinegar, and other ground chilies.

# Your Shopping List:

- ❑ 1 28-oz. can of crushed tomatoes in puree
- ❑ 1 14-oz. can of beef broth
- ❑ 1 7-oz. can of chipoltes in adobo sauce

## From Your Pantry:

- ❑ vegetable oil, garlic, brown sugar, molasses, cider vinegar, Worcestershire sauce, ground cloves, ground cinnamon

# Basil & Balsamic Vinegar Sauce

| | |
|---|---|
| 1 c. | balsamic vinegar |
| 2 T. | honey |
| 1 T. | olive oil |
| 2 T. | fresh basil, chopped |
| 2 T. | fresh Italian flat-leaf parsley, chopped |
| 2 t. | freshly ground black pepper |

In a small saucepan, combine the vinegar, honey, oil and half of the basil, parsley and black pepper. Over medium-high heat bring this to a boil, then reduce the heat to medium-low and simmer for 15 minutes. The sauce should thicken. Stir in the remaining basil, parsley, and pepper. Brush this sauce on during the last 15 minutes of grilling. The sauce can be refrigerated for up to a week. Makes about 1 cup.

Kids can help with this recipe:

1. Clean the basil and parsley and remove the leaves from their stems.

2. Measure the vinegar, honey, oil, 1 tablespoon of basil, 1 tablespoon of parsley, and 1 teaspoon of black pepper, and place in an unheated small saucepan.

3. Measure 1 tablespoon of basil, 1 tablespoon of parsley, and 1 teaspoon of black pepper.

**Teachable Moment:** If you have a good selection of vinegars in your pantry, show them to your child helper and talk about their differences. Explain that you will be using balsamic vinegar in this dish. Balsamic vinegar is made from sweet white grapes that are boiled to create syrup. This syrup is put in wooden barrels to "age" and they take on the flavors of the wood. To be called "balsamic," the vinegar must be made in the Modena and Reggio regions of Italy. Balsamic vinegar has a sweet taste and can be used in dressings, marinades, and even drizzled over strawberries and ice cream!

## quick tip

This is an excellent sauce for barbecued fish, such as halibut or salmon. You could also use this sauce on poultry as a marinade or as a basting sauce. It is also excellent drizzled over roasted or barbecued vegetables.

# Your Shopping List:

- [ ] 1 bunch of fresh basil
- [ ] 1 bunch of fresh Italian flat-leaf parsley

## From Your Pantry:

- [ ] balsamic vinegar, honey, extra-virgin olive oil, black pepper

# Orange Mustard Sauce

| | |
|---|---|
| 1/2 c. | orange marmalade |
| 1/2 c. | Dijon mustard |
| 1/3 c. | fresh orange juice |
| 1 t. | dried rosemary |
| 1/2 t. | celery seed |
| 1 t. | orange zest, grated |

In a small saucepan, combine the marmalade, mustard, orange juice, rosemary, celery seed, and orange zest. Over medium-low heat bring the sauce to a simmer, stirring often until the sauce is slightly thickened (about 8 minutes). Brush the sauce on your choice of meat during the last 10 minutes of grilling. The sauce can be refrigerated for a week. Makes about 1-1/2 cups.

Kids can help with this recipe:

1. With a child-safe zester or rasp, zest the orange.

2. Measure all of the ingredients and place in a small saucepan.

# Your Shopping List:

- [ ] 1 18-oz. jar of orange marmalade
- [ ] 1 half-pint fresh orange juice
- [ ] 1 fresh orange, for its zest

## From Your Pantry:

- [ ] Dijon mustard, dried rosemary, celery seed

## quick tip

The combination of orange and beef always produces a fantastic flavor. This sauce is an excellent flavor enhancer for all barbecue-ready cuts of beef. You can marinate the beef in half of the sauce for 1 hour before grilling, and then use the remaining sauce to baste the meat as it grills.

# Sweet and Peppery Peanut Sauce

| | |
|---|---|
| 3 T. | peanut oil |
| 1 c. | onions, minced |
| 2 c. | chunky peanut butter |
| 2 c. | chicken broth |
| 2 T. | brown sugar |
| 2 T. | cider vinegar |
| 1/2 t. | cayenne pepper |

In a medium saucepan, sauté the onions in the peanut oil until they are soft. Add the peanut butter, chicken broth, brown sugar, cider vinegar, and cayenne pepper. Blend well. Over medium-low heat, simmer the sauce for 10 to 15 minutes, stirring frequently to prevent the sauce from sticking to the bottom of the pan. This sauce can be refrigerated for up to a week. Makes about 2-1/2 cups of sauce.

Kids can help with this recipe:

1. Measure the peanut oil.

2. Older kids can, with supervision, open the can of chicken broth with a can opener.

3. Measure the peanut butter, chicken broth, brown sugar, cider vinegar, and cayenne pepper.

**Teachable Moment:** This sauce provides a great opportunity to discuss one of your child helper's favorite foods: peanut butter. Peanuts originated in South America and spread throughout the world with the travels of European explorers. The Incas made the first peanut butter, crushing the nuts to form a paste-like substance. George Washington Carver, an African-American scientist, re-invented peanut butter in the 1880s as well as 300 other uses for peanuts. He popularized peanuts and they became a major crop in the South.

# Your Shopping List:

- ❑ 1 large yellow onion
- ❑ 1 18-oz. jar of chunky peanut butter
- ❑ 1 14-oz. can of chicken broth

## From Your Pantry:

- ❑ peanut oil, brown sugar, cider vinegar, cayenne pepper

# quick tip

This spicy sauce is a delicious accompaniment to Southeast Asian-style stir-fries and skewered, barbecue meats. Make a quick chicken satay by threading chicken tenders on skewers, grilling until done, and drizzling with this luscious sauce. It is something both kids and guests will love!

# Maple Spice Sauce

| 1 c. | maple syrup |
| 2 T. | butter |
| 2-1/2 T. | fresh lemon juice |
| 1 t. | ground cinnamon |
| 1/2 t. | ground allspice |
| 1/4 t. | ground nutmeg |
| 1/4 t. | ground cloves |

In a small saucepan over medium heat, simmer the maple syrup for 10 minutes until it has reduced to about 3/4 cup. Stir in the butter, let it melt, and remove the saucepan from the heat. Cool. Stir in the lemon juice, cinnamon, allspice, nutmeg, and cloves, blending well. This sauce can be refrigerated for up to a week. To use, reheat the sauce to melt the butter. Makes about 1 cup.

Kids can help with this recipe:

1. Measure the maple syrup.

2. Measure the butter.

3. Squeeze the lemons for their juice. Remove any seeds.

4. Measure the lemon juice and spices.

# Your Shopping List:

❏  3 lemons, for their juice

## From Your Pantry:

❏  maple syrup, butter, ground cinnamon, ground allspice, ground nutmeg, ground cloves

## quick tip

Drizzle this earthy sauce onto sliced, cooked turkey or pork. It enhances the flavors of these meats with its sweet spice. Also use this sauce when baking butternut squash or pumpkin; baste it over the cut pieces as they roast in the oven. Another great use is to flavor mashed sweet potatoes.

# Garlic Lemon Caper Sauce

| | |
|---|---|
| 1/2 c. | fresh lemon juice |
| 3 T. | extra-virgin olive oil |
| 6 cloves | garlic, minced |
| 1/4 c. | green onions, minced |
| 1 T. | lemon zest |
| 1 t. | ground black pepper |
| 1/4 c. | small capers, drained |

In a nonreactive bowl, whisk together the lemon juice and the olive oil. Add and stir together until the garlic, green onions, lemon zest, black pepper, and the capers are well blended. Cover and refrigerate for at least 2 hours before using. This sauce can be refrigerated for up to 4 days. Makes about 1 cup.

Kids can help with this recipe:

1. Using a child-safe zester, zest enough lemons to yield 1 tablespoon of zest.

2. Squeeze the lemons for their juice and remove any seeds.

3. Measure the lemon juice and olive oil. Whisk together.

4. Mince the garlic with a garlic press.

5. Measure the green onions, black pepper, and capers. Add to the lemon juice mixture along with the garlic and lemon zest.

**Teachable Moment:** Capers are the unopened flower buds of a Mediterranean bush. They are harvested, sun-dried, and placed in strong brine or in salt.

# Your Shopping List:

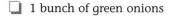

- ☐ 5 to 6 fresh lemons, for their juice and zest
- ☐ 1 bunch of green onions

## From Your Pantry:

- ☐ extra-virgin olive oil, garlic, black pepper, non-pareil capers

## quick tip

This is the ultimate seafood sauce. Drizzle over grilled fish or shellfish for a sophisticated, lemony taste. Garnish with minced parsley for color.

## Tomato & Chile Salsa

| | |
|---|---|
| 2 c. | ripe tomatoes, peeled, seeded and chopped |
| 1 c. | minced onion |
| 1 T. | fresh lime juice |
| 3 T. | fresh tomato juice |
| 2 T. | fresh cilantro, minced |
| 1 T. | small green chilies, minced |
| 2 cloves | garlic, pressed |
| 2 t. | chili powder |
| 1 t. | ground black pepper |
| 1/2 t. | salt |

In a nonreactive bowl, combine the tomatoes, onion, lime juice, tomato juice, cilantro, chilies, pressed garlic, chili powder, black pepper, and salt. Toss gently, cover, and refrigerate for at least 2 hours to let the flavors mingle. Serve fresh. This salsa can be refrigerated for up to 3 days, but it tastes best on the day that it is made. Makes about 3-1/2 cups.

Kids can help with this recipe:

1. Squeeze the limes for their juice.
2. Wash the tomatoes and cilantro.
3. Mince the garlic in a garlic press.
4. Measure the tomatoes, onion, lime juice, tomato juice, cilantro, chilies, garlic, chili powder, black pepper, and salt, and combine them in a non-reactive bowl.

## Your Shopping List:

- ❑ 3 medium ripe tomatoes
- ❑ 1 large red onion
- ❑ 2 ripe limes, for their juice
- ❑ 1 half-pint fresh tomato juice
- ❑ 1 bunch of fresh cilantro
- ❑ 1 jalapeño pepper

### From Your Pantry:

- ❑ garlic, chili powder, black pepper, salt

## quick tip

Salsa is a Tex-Mex classic and can be used as an appetizer with tortilla chips or as a condiment for tacos, burritos, and quesadillas. For a twist, try adding chunks of avocado or even chopped, ripe melon or nectarines for a little sweetness.

# Jicama-Citrus Salsa

| | |
|---|---|
| 1-1/2 c. | jicama, peeled and finely chopped |
| 1 c. | orange slices, peeled and finely chopped |
| 1/4 c. | fresh Italian flat-leaf parsley, minced |
| 1/4 c. | fresh orange juice |
| 1 T. | white vinegar |
| 1 t. | jalapeño peppers, minced |
| 1/2 t. | ground black pepper |
| 1/2 t. | salt |

Combine the jicama, orange, parsley, orange juice, vinegar, jalapeño peppers, pepper, and salt in a nonreactive bowl. Stir gently to blend. Cover and chill for at least 2 hours for the flavors to blend. Refrigerate for up to 2 days. The salsa is best when served the day it is made. Makes about 3 cups.

Kids can help with this recipe:

1. Peel the orange.
2. Wash the parsley.
3. Measure all of the ingredients and combine in a non-reactive bowl.

**Teachable Moment:** Let your child helper handle the unpeeled jicama and explain that it is also known as the "Mexican potato" or "Mexican turnip." The skin must be peeled before eating the crunchy, white interior. The taste is similar to that of a water chestnut.

# Your Shopping List:

- ☐ 1 large jicama
- ☐ 1 large orange
- ☐ 1 half-pint fresh orange juice
- ☐ 1 jalapeño pepper

## From Your Pantry:

- ☐ white vinegar, black pepper, salt

**quick tip**

This citrus salsa complements poultry, especially chicken. Simply grill boneless, skinless chicken breasts and top with this delightful salsa.

# Tomatillo Salsa Verde

| | |
|---|---|
| 1-1/2 c. | tomatillos, chopped |
| 1/4 c. | white onion, chopped |
| 2 T. | serrano chile, seeded and diced |
| 1 T. | fresh cilantro, minced |
| 2 T. | fresh parsley, minced |
| 3 cloves | garlic, pressed |
| 1/2 t. | salt |
| 1 t. | ground black pepper |
| 1/2 t. | crushed red pepper |
| 2 T. | white vinegar |
| 2 T. | water |

Using a food processor or blender, place the tomatillos, onion, chile, cilantro, parsley, garlic, salt, black pepper, red pepper, and vinegar into the bowl. Puree the mixture, adding the water a little at a time. Adjust the seasonings to taste and let it stand for at least 1 hour. The salsa may be refrigerated for up to 3 days. It tastes best when served on the day it was made. Makes about 2 cups.

Kids can help with this recipe:

1. Wash the tomatillos and remove any husks.

2. Wash the cilantro and parsley.

3. Measure all the ingredients and place in the bowl of a food processor.

**Teachable Moment:** Tomatillos are related to tomatoes and are also known as the Mexican green tomato. They are a small, green fruit that is enclosed in a thin, papery husk. Native to Mexico, they are used in Mexican and Southwestern cuisine (both cooked and raw).

**quick tip**

Although making this salsa is extremely easy, you can also buy high-quality salsa verde in the supermarket. The best salsa verde is refrigerated, not jarred or canned. One exceptionally easy dish is to simmer pork butt or shoulder in the salsa verde until it is falling off the bone. Shred the scrumptious meat and serve with beans, rice, and tortillas.

# Your Shopping List:

- ❑ 1-1/2 c. tomatillos
- ❑ 1 small white onion
- ❑ 2 serrano chiles
- ❑ 1 bunch of fresh cilantro
- ❑ 1 bunch of fresh Italian flat-leaf parsley

## From Your Pantry:

- ❑ garlic, salt, black pepper, crushed red pepper, white vinegar

# Pineapple Peach Salsa

| | |
|---|---|
| 1 c. | fresh pineapple, finely chopped |
| 1 c. | fresh peach, peeled and chopped |
| 2 T. | green onion, finely chopped |
| 2 T. | pineapple juice (juice reserved from the fresh pineapple) |
| 1/4 c. | white wine vinegar |
| 1/4 c. | honey |
| 2 T. | fresh Italian flat-leaf parsley, minced |
| 1 clove | garlic, pressed |
| 1/2 t. | salt |

Combine the pineapple, peaches, green onion, pineapple juice, white wine vinegar, honey, parsley, garlic, and salt, gently stirring to blend well. Cover the bowl and refrigerate for at least 2 hours. Best when served on the day this salsa is made. It can be refrigerated for up to 2 days. Makes about 2-1/2 cups.

Kids can help with this recipe:

1. Wash the peaches.
2. Measure the green onion, pineapple juice, white wine vinegar, honey, parsley, garlic, and salt. Combine with the pineapple.

**quick tip**

This sweet salsa is a perfect match for ham and rich fish, such as salmon. If fresh pineapple is unavailable, use a high-quality canned pineapple.

# Your Shopping List:

- [ ] 1 whole pineapple (for its flesh and juice)
- [ ] 2 medium fresh peaches
- [ ] 1 bunch of green onion
- [ ] 1 bunch of fresh Italian flat-leaf parsley

## From Your Pantry:

- [ ] white wine vinegar, honey, garlic, salt

# Rum & Molasses Marinade

| | |
|---|---|
| 1/2 c. | cider vinegar |
| 1/3 c. | dark molasses |
| 1/2 c. | vegetable oil |
| 1/4 c. | rum |
| 1/4 t. | ground black pepper |
| 1 clove | garlic, minced |
| 1 T. | fresh parsley, minced |

In a small bowl, whisk together the vinegar, molasses, oil, and the rum until smooth and well blended. Stir in the black pepper, garlic and the parsley. Makes about 1-1/2 cups.

Kids can help with this recipe:

1. Measure and whisk together the vinegar, molasses, oil, and rum.

2. Mince the garlic in a garlic press.

3. Wash the parsley.

4. Measure the black pepper and add to the mixture.

5. Add the garlic and parsley.

## quick tip

This marinade is the perfect way to flavor beef or pork. Place the meat in a shallow dish and pour the marinade over the meat. Turn the meat once and cover it. Refrigerate for at least 5 hours or overnight. Turn the meat occasionally. Cook as you like.

**Teachable Moment:** Molasses is made when sugarcane juices are boiled to extract the sugar crystals to form table sugar. The remaining liquid is light molasses. When this is boiled a second time, it becomes much darker and thicker and is known as dark molasses.

# Your Shopping List:

❑  1 bunch of fresh Italian flat-leaf parsley

## From Your Pantry:

❑  cider vinegar, dark molasses, vegetable oil, rum, black pepper, garlic

# Fresh Herb Marinade

| | |
|---|---|
| 1/2 c. | rice wine vinegar |
| 1/4 c. | fresh lemon juice |
| 2 T. | vegetable oil |
| 2 t. | lemon zest |
| 1 T. | fresh basil, minced |
| 1 T. | fresh parsley, minced |
| 1 T. | fresh thyme, minced |
| 1/4 t. | ground black pepper |

In a small bowl, whisk together the vinegar, lemon juice, and oil until smooth and blended. Add the zest, basil, parsley, thyme, and black pepper, and stir to mix well. Makes about 1 cup.

## quick tip

The bright, fresh flavors of this marinade marry well with seafood and pork. Pour this over the seafood that has been placed in a shallow glass dish. Turn the seafood once, cover the dish and refrigerate for about 30 minutes. Turn the seafood occasionally as it marinates. Marinate pork for 1 to 2 hours. Grill or roast as you like.

Kids can help with this recipe:

1. Zest the lemons with a child-safe zester to yield 2 teaspoons zest.
2. Squeeze the lemons for their juice. Remove any seeds.
3. Measure the vinegar, lemon juice, and vegetable oil. Whisk together until smooth.
4. Wash the fresh herbs and remove the leaves from their stems.
5. Add the zest to the lemon juice mixture.
6. Measure the fresh herbs and black pepper. Add to the lemon juice mixture.

## Your Shopping List:

- ❑ 3 to 4 fresh lemons, for their juice and zest
- ❑ 1 bunch of fresh basil
- ❑ 1 bunch of fresh Italian flat-leaf parsley
- ❑ 1 bunch of fresh thyme

## From Your Pantry:

- ❑ rice wine vinegar, vegetable oil, black pepper

## Snappy Citrus Marinade

| | |
|---|---|
| 5 cloves | garlic, minced |
| 1/2 t. | salt |
| 2 t. | dried oregano |
| 1/2 t. | ground cumin |
| 1/3 c. | red wine vinegar |
| 1/3 c. | fresh orange juice |
| 1/3 c. | fresh lime juice |
| 2 T. | vegetable oil |
| 1/4 c. | fresh parsley, minced |
| 1/4 t. | ground black pepper |

Mash the garlic with the salt to make a paste. Scrape this into a small bowl and stir in the oregano and the cumin. Blend well. Whisk in the vinegar, orange juice, lime juice, vegetable oil, parsley, and black pepper until completely mixed. Makes about 1 cup.

Kids can help with this recipe:

1. Mince the garlic in a garlic press. Combine the salt with the garlic and mash with a fork.

2. Measure the oregano and cumin and add to the garlic paste.

3. Squeeze the limes for their juice.

4. Wash the parsley and remove the leaves from their stems.

5. Measure the vinegar, orange juice, lime juice, vegetable oil, parsley, and black pepper. Add to the garlic mixture. Mix completely.

# Your Shopping List:

❏ 1 half-pint fresh orange juice
❏ 3 fresh limes, for their juice
❏ 1 bunch of fresh Italian flat-leaf parsley

## From Your Pantry:

❏ garlic, salt, dried oregano, ground cumin, red wine vinegar, vegetable oil, black pepper

## quick tip

This zesty, versatile marinade is a nice partner with fish, chicken, or pork. Place the meat in a shallow baking dish and pour the marinade over the meat. Turn the meat once and cover the dish. Refrigerate while marinating the meat. Marinate 30 minutes to 1 hour for fish and 1 to 2 hours for chicken or pork. Cook using your favorite method.

# Fruit and Curry Sauce

| | |
|---|---|
| 4 T. | butter |
| 1 small | onion, chopped |
| 1 small | apple, peeled and chopped |
| 1/2 | banana, chopped |
| 2 T. | mango chutney |
| 1 t. | curry powder |
| 1 c. | chicken broth |

In a large skillet over medium heat, melt the butter. Add the onion, apple, banana, chutney and the curry powder. Cook for 3 minutes, until the onion is translucent. Add the chicken broth to the skillet and bring the sauce to a boil. Reduce the heat to low and simmer for 5 minutes. Remove the skillet from the heat and allow the sauce to cool slightly. In a blender, process the cooled sauce until it is smooth. Return the sauce to the skillet over medium heat and warm just until simmering.

You may use this sauce hot or cold. After the sauce simmers, you may ladle this sauce over any fish or chicken that has been grilled and serve. To serve this sauce cold, pour the simmered sauce into a bowl, cover and refrigerate for 2 hours. The cold sauce can be used as a dipping sauce for vegetables, fruit or cold meats and seafood. Makes about 2 cups.

Kids can help with this recipe:

1. Measure and place the butter in the cold skillet.
2. Peel and chop the banana with child-friendly knife
3. Measure the chutney and curry powder
4. Older kids, can with supervision, open the can of chicken broth with a can opener.

**Teachable Moment:** Curry powder is a mixture of different spices. The main spice is turmeric. All of the spices in curry are known from early times for improving the way our brains work.

# Your Shopping List:

- ☐ 1 small onion
- ☐ 1 apple
- ☐ 1 banana
- ☐ 1 small jar mango chutney

## From Your Pantry:

- ☐ butter, curry powder and chicken broth

# Hawaiian Sweet & Sour Sauce

| | |
|---|---|
| 2 T. | vegetable oil |
| 1 clove | garlic, minced |
| 1/2 c. | reserved pineapple juice (add water if necessary to make 1/2 cup) |
| 1/4 c. | rice vinegar |
| 2 T. | ketchup |
| 2 T. | soy sauce |
| 1/4 t. | crushed red pepper |
| 2 T. | cornstarch |
| 2 T. | water |
| 1 7 oz. | can crushed pineapple, juices drained and reserved |

In a skillet over medium heat, heat the oil and lightly brown the garlic. Add the pineapple juice, vinegar, ketchup, soy sauce, cornstarch and water. Stir to mix thoroughly and reduce the heat to low. Simmer until the sauce is thickened. Add the pineapple and heat through. Serve this sauce hot to be ladled over grilled meats or use as a sauce for stir-fry. Makes about 2 cups.

Kids can help with this recipe:

1. Measure and pour the oil into a cold skillet
2. Measure and mix together in a separate bowl, the pineapple juice, vinegar, ketchup, soy sauce, cornstarch and water.

**Teachable Moment:** Soy sauce is said to have been started by a priest from China who was living in Japan in 1250. He noticed that when the soybean paste is fermented, it produces a liquid that has a delicious flavor, soy sauce. Most of the soy sauce that we use today is still made in Japan.

# Your Shopping List:

❑ 1 7-oz. can crushed pineapple

# From Your Pantry:

❑ garlic, rice vinegar, ketchup, soy sauce, red pepper and cornstarch

# Lemongrass & Ginger Grilling Sauce

| | |
|---|---|
| 1/4 c. | sugar |
| 1 T. | cornstarch |
| 1 1/4 c. | low-sodium chicken broth |
| 1/2 c. | rice vinegar |
| 3 T. | Thai fish sauce |
| 2 T. | fresh ginger, minced |
| 2 T. | lemongrass, chopped (you may substitute 1 t. grated lemon zest) |
| 1/2 t. | crushed hot pepper flakes |
| 1 t. | dried basil |

In a small saucepan, combine together the sugar and cornstarch. Whisk in the chicken broth, vinegar, fish sauce, ginger, lemongrass, pepper flakes and the basil. Bring the sauce to a boil stirring constantly, and cook for 1 minute. The sauce will thicken slightly. Reduce the heat and simmer for 2 to 3 minutes. Remove the sauce from the heat. Because this sauce has sugar in it, brush it on your meat during the last 8 to 10 minutes of grilling to make a shiny, caramelized glaze. Makes 1-3/4 cup.

Kids can help with this recipe:

1. Measure and stir together the sugar and cornstarch.
2. Measure and stir in the broth, vinegar, fish sauce, ginger, lemongrass and basil.

# Your Shopping List:

- ☐ 1 jar Thai fish sauce
- ☐ 1 small piece fresh ginger
- ☐ 1 small bunch lemongrass

## From Your Pantry:

- ☐ sugar, cornstarch, chicken broth, rice vinegar, hot pepper flakes, dried basil

## quick tip

You may make this sauce up to a week ahead and refrigerate it. When you get home from a busy day, place your meat on the grill, bring the sauce to room temperature and brush it on the grilling meat to glaze.

# Lemon & Thyme Aioli

| | |
|---|---|
| 3/4 c. | lowfat plain yogurt |
| 1/2 c. | mayonnaise |
| 1 T. | fresh lemon juice |
| 2 t. | grated lemon zest |
| 2 cloves | garlic, minced |
| | salt and white pepper to taste |
| 1 t. | fresh thyme, minced |

In a blender, process the yogurt and mayonnaise together until smooth. Spoon out into a refrigerator bowl with lid. Add the fresh lemon juice, lemon zest, garlic, salt and pepper and the thyme. Stir to combine thoroughly. Cover the aioli and refrigerate for 1 hour or up to 6 hours. Use the chilled aioli as a drizzle over freshly cooked asparagus, broccoli, and other vegetables. Use as a sauce over freshly cooked fish and poultry. Makes about 1 cup.

Kids can help with this recipe:

1. Measure the yogurt and mayonnaise and spoon into the blender.
2. Squeeze the lemons for fresh juice.
3. Remove the thyme leaves from the sprig.
4. Measure and stir together the lemon juice, zest, garlic, salt and pepper and the thyme with the yogurt and mayonnaise.

**Teachable Moments:** Thyme is an herb originally from the Mediterranean. The first colonists brought thyme over to use as a food preservative and as medicine. Thyme was used in Egypt to help preserve the mummies.

# Your Shopping List:

- ❑ 1 8-oz. container lowfat yogurt
- ❑ 2 lemons for fresh juice and zest
- ❑ 1 small container white pepper
- ❑ 1 sprig fresh thyme

## From Your Pantry:

- ❑ mayonnaise, garlic, salt

# Zesty Ginger Sweet & Sour Sauce

| | |
|---|---|
| 2 T. | rice wine vinegar |
| 1/4 c. | dark Asian sesame oil |
| 1/4 t. | ground ginger |
| 1 t. | brown sugar |
| 1/4 t. | cayenne pepper |

Combine all ingredients in a shaker jar or plastic container. Cover tightly and shake or whisk until smooth. Store the sauce in the refrigerator for up to 1 week. Makes about 1/4 cup.

Kids can help with this recipe:

1. Measure the liquids: rice wine vinegar and sesame oil.
2. Measure the sugar and dry spices: ginger and cayenne pepper.
3. Shake the jar or plastic container until the sauce is well-blended.

## From Your Pantry:

☐ Rice wine vinegar, Asian sesame oil, ground ginger, brown sugar, cayenne pepper

## quick tip

For a super-fast entrée, combine this sauce with cooked, chopped chicken and serve over hot soba noodles or brown rice. Sprinkle with sesame seeds and serve. Also great over spinach or cucumbers and tomatoes!

# Roasted Garlic & Red Pepper Aioli

| | |
|---|---|
| 2 large heads | garlic, peeled |
| 2 T. | red bell pepper, finely minced |
| 2 t. | extra-virgin olive oil |
| 3/4 c. | lowfat mayonnaise |
| 2 T. | extra-virgin olive oil |
| 2 t. | fresh lemon juice |
| 1 t. | Dijon mustard |

Preheat the oven to 325ºF. Place the whole garlic heads and the red pepper in a shallow baking dish. Drizzle with 2 teaspoons of the olive oil. Bake about 40 minutes, or until very soft. Stir once or twice as needed.

To prepare the aioli, squeeze the roasted garlic cloves from each head of garlic. Place the roasted garlic and pepper bits in a small bowl. Add the mayonnaise, remaining olive oil, lemon juice and mustard. Whisk to combine. Serve with baked potatoes, linguine with broccoli, or mixed vegetables. Makes about 3/4 cup aioli.

Kids can help with this recipe:

1. Rub the garlic skins away from the garlic.
2. Drizzle the oil over the garlic and red pepper.
3. Measure the olive oil, lemon juice, mayonnaise and mustard.
4. Older kids can, with supervision, whisk the aioli to blend.

**Teachable Moment:** Aioli is a garlic sauce originally from the south of France. It is best made by hand using a mortar and pestle to grind the garlic and spices into a paste. Oil is then added slowly to blend all together into a mayonnaise-like sauce.

# Your Shopping List:

- ☐ 2 heads garlic
- ☐ 1 red bell pepper
- ☐ 1 fresh lemon

## From Your Pantry:

- ☐ extra-virgin olive oil, reduced-fat mayonnaise, Dijon mustard

# quick tip

Roast several cloves of garlic at a time and store roasted garlic cloves in the refrigerator for up to 2 weeks.

# Artichoke & Sun-Dried Tomato Sauce

| | |
|---|---|
| 12-oz. jar | roasted red peppers, with liquid |
| 6-oz. jar | marinated artichoke hearts, with liquid |
| 1/4 c. | sun-dried tomatoes, drained |
| 2 T. | fresh parsley, minced |
| 1 t. | fresh basil, minced |
| 2 large | beefsteak tomatoes, chopped |
| 1 T. | extra-virgin olive oil |
| 1/2 t. | salt |
| 1/2 t. | coarsely ground black pepper |

Place the red peppers with liquid, artichoke hearts with liquid, sun-dried tomatoes and herbs in a blender. Pulse for 1 minute until smooth. Pour over the beefsteak tomatoes and add the olive oil, salt and pepper. Mix lightly and let stand for 5 minutes. To serve, spoon over hot, cooked pasta or use as a hearty spread for thick slices of peasant bread. Makes about 1-1/2 cups.

Kids can help with this recipe:

1. Place the peppers, artichokes, sun-dried tomatoes and herbs in the blender.
2. Wash the fresh tomatoes and herbs. Pat dry.
3. Measure the the oil, salt and pepper.

# Your Shopping List:

- ❏ 12-oz. jar roasted red peppers
- ❏ 6-oz. jar marinated artichoke hearts
- ❏ 4-oz. jar sun-dried tomatoes
- ❏ 1 bunch fresh parsley
- ❏ 1 bunch fresh basil
- ❏ 2 large beefsteak tomatoes

## From Your Pantry:

- ❏ extra-virgin olive oil, salt and pepper

## quick tip

Purchase tomatoes when they are very fresh during the summer months. Chop and place approximately one cup of tomatoes in several small, self-sealing plastic bags. Freeze and use as needed.

# Parsley & Walnut Pesto

| | |
|---|---|
| 1 c. | fresh parsley leaves, cleaned and tightly packed |
| 1/4 c. | walnuts, roughly chopped |
| 2 T. | fresh lemon juice |
| 2 T. | extra-virgin olive oil |

Place all of the ingredients in a food processor blender and pulse until pureed. Use as a sauce for fresh steamed vegetables or hot, cooked pasta. Makes 2/3 cup.

Kids can help with this recipe:

1. Kids of all ages can pack the parsley leaves in a dry ingredient measuring cup.

2. Measure the walnuts, lemon juice and olive oil.

# Your Shopping List:

- ❏ 1 bunch fresh parsley
- ❏ 4-oz. bag chopped walnuts
- ❏ 1 fresh lemon

## From Your Pantry:

- ❏ extra-virgin olive oil

## quick tip

Dice 2 large ham steaks into small pieces. Add to 4 cups hot, cooked pasta and pour the pesto over all. Toss and serve immediately. Serves 4.

# Pan Pacific Vinaigrette

| | |
|---|---|
| 1/2 c. | extra-virgin olive oil |
| 1 T. | fresh lemon juice |
| 1/4 c. | fresh cilantro, minced |
| 1 T. | garlic, minced |
| 1 t. | ground cumin |
| 1/2 t. | ground paprika |
| 1/2 t. | salt |
| 1/4 t. | black pepper |

Place all ingredients in a blender and blend until smooth. Makes about 3/4 cup.

Kids can help with this recipe:

1. Measure the oil.

2. Squeeze the lemon and measure the juice.

3. Measure the garlic and spices.

# Your Shopping List:

❑ 1 lemon for fresh juice
❑ 1 bunch fresh cilantro

## From Your Pantry:

❑ extra virgin olive oil, garlic, cumin, paprika, salt and pepper

## quick tip

Pour this vinaigrette over almost any combination of pasta or rice and cooked meat and vegetables. Try adding 4 cups hot, cooked brown or white rice and top with shredded, cooked chicken breast. Add cooked peas or carrot slices and garnish with parsley.

# Mustard Sauce Made for Fruits & Vegetables

| | |
|---|---|
| 1/2 c. | crumbled silken tofu |
| 1/4 c. | canola oil |
| 2 T. | pure maple syrup |
| 2 T. | water |
| 1 T. | Dijon mustard |
| 1/4 t. | dry mustard |
| | salt and pepper to taste |

Combine all of the ingredients in a blender or food processor fitted with the metal blade. Process until the sauce is creamy. Chill. Makes about 2/3 cups.

This sauce can be used on fresh fruit salad, steamed veggies or as a dressing for coleslaw. Its sweet and mild flavor is a unique addition to fruits and vegetables.

Kids can help with this recipe:

1. Crumble the tofu into the blender or food processor.
2. Measure and pour the canola oil, maple syrup and water.
3. Measure and add both mustards.

**Teachable Moment:** What is tofu? It is made from soy milk and soy milk is made from soy beans. Like cheese is to milk...tofu is to soy milk. It is very healthful and can be used instead of dairy products.

# Your Shopping List:

❑  1 small package silken tofu

# From Your Pantry:

❑  canola oil, maple syrup, Dijon mustard, dry mustard and salt and pepper

# Raspberry Vinaigrette

| | |
|---|---|
| 1/4 c. | extra-virgin olive oil |
| 3 T. | seedless raspberry jelly |
| 3 T. | wine vinegar |
| 1 t. | garlic, crushed |
| 1/4 t. | salt |
| | pepper to taste |

Combine all of the ingredients in a blender and process until smooth. Use this vinaigrette on steamed green leafy vegetables or fresh salad. It also gives citrus fruits an added zing. Makes 2/3 cup.

Kids can help with this recipe:

1. Measure and pour into the blender the olive oil, raspberry jelly and vinegar.
2. Crush garlic using the back of a spoon on a wood cutting board.

# Your Shopping List:

☐ 1 6-oz. jar seedless raspberry jelly

# From Your Pantry:

☐ extra virgin olive oil, wine vinegar, garlic, salt and pepper

# Fresh Italian Dressing

| | |
|---|---|
| 1/4 c. | extra-virgin olive oil |
| 2 T. | wine vinegar |
| 1 T. | fresh lemon juice |
| 2 t. | Dijon mustard |
| 1/2 t. | sugar |
| 1/2 t. | crushed garlic |
| 1/2 t. | dried basil |
| 1/2 t. | dried oregano |
| 1 leaf | fresh basil and oregano, minced |

Combine the ingredients except the fresh herbs, in a small bowl and whisk together until emulsified. Stir in the fresh basil and oregano. This is excellent on pasta salad or an antipasto plate. Makes 1/2 cup.

Kids can help with this recipe:

1. Measure the olive oil and vinegar into the small bowl.
2. Squeeze the lemon for the fresh juice
3. Measure and add into the bowl the mustard, sugar, dried basil and dried oregano.
4. Crush the garlic using a spoon on a cutting board.
5. Older children can whisk together the ingredients until smooth.

# Your Shopping List:

- ❑ 1 fresh lemon for juice
- ❑ 1 small bunch fresh basil
- ❑ 1 small bunch fresh oregano

## From Your Pantry:

- ❑ olive oil, wine vinegar, Dijon mustard, sugar, garlic, dried basil and dried oregano

## quick tip

To quickly mince fresh herbs, roll each leaf tightly. Slice the roll thinly and finish with a few quick chops.

# Index

## Y

**Yogurt**
    Creamy Berry Smoothie, 42
    Lemon & Thyme Aioli, 185
    Pineapple & Banana Smoothie,
        140

## Z

**Zesty Ginger Sweet & Sour
    Sauce, 186**
**Ziti, Chicken & Zucchini,
    55–56**
**Zucchini**
    Chicken & Zucchini Ziti, 55–56
    Pasta e Fagioli, 50–51